Big Red/Channel Bass Fishing

Big Red/
Channel Bass Fishing

A. C. Becker, Jr.

South Brunswick and New York: A. S. Barnes and Company
London: Thomas Yoseloff Ltd

A. S. Barnes and Co., Inc.
Cranbury, New Jersey 08512

Thomas Yoseloff Ltd
108 New Bond Street
London W1Y OQX, England

ISBN 0-498-07826-4
Printed in the United States of America

Contents

Author's Note

A fellow does not have to catch a huge fish to enjoy the sport of angling. If his tackle is balanced to the size of fish caught, he can have as much sport in landing an eight-pound largemouth bass as in taking a 100-pound tarpon. Unfortunately with most big fish the cost of catching them rises in direct proportions to the size. In this day of the shrinking dollar, this means the fellow on the fixed income has to budget his trips for the big ones.

This is not the case when it comes to the channel bass, a muscular salt-water brawler known equally well by the name redfish. In terms of money, sports fishing for redfish is economical. Costly and specialized tackle and expensive boats are not necessary to get into the action where the big ones are.

Tens of thousands of these great gamefish, tackle-busters in excess of 25 pounds, are caught annually from piers, jetties, and the surf. There is an expense involved in channel bass fishing, but rather than money it is an expense in time. If a fisherman is to be successful in consistently catching redfish, he must be willing to spend the time to learn all the habits and characteristics of this fine fish. There is far, far more to catching it than just tossing a baited hook into the water. After the knowledge is gained, the fisherman must be willing to spend additional time, often long hours, in waiting out the strikes.

This story of the channel bass is also a story of ecology and environment. Some dire things have been predicted for man unless he takes immediate and effective steps to cure the ills of pollution and stops the indiscriminate use of insecticides. In this book I have sought to point out how the average fisherman can enjoy big-game sports fishing for a modest price, and at the same time be concerned with the environmental problems.

Just a few decades ago—or more specifically, before World War II—redfish were extremely plentiful from Tampico, Mexico, to the fringe of Massachusetts. The petro-chemical and industrial expansions spurred after World War II and the urbanization of much of our coastlines have changed the picture. Some areas that once abounded with fish are today relatively sterile. Overall the redfish population is still high and it does not look like we are going to "run out of reds" in the near future. Nevertheless, the shrinking range of this fish and the destruction of some areas that were natural channel bass havens should be sufficient cause for sportsmen to show concern for the future.

The purpose of this book is to bring under one cover all the information available on the channel bass. Prior to submission to the publisher, this material was read by a number of fishermen—commercials as well as sports anglers—for criticisms and verification of facts and information presented. Some of the criticisms, of course, necessitated alterations and revisions.

In preparing this book the author received valuable aid and material from state game and fish departments of Texas, Louisiana, Mississippi, Alabama, Florida, South Carolina, North Carolina, Virginia, Maryland, New Jersey, and New York, as well as the Bureau of Sports Fisheries of the U. S. Fish and Wildlife Service.

Special credit for research assistance and encouragement in completing the project must be extended to Howard Robbins, veteran operator of Texas fishing piers and a lifelong channel bass angler, who has caught his share of big redfish all the way from the Atlantic Seaboard through the Gulf Coast.

A. C. Becker, Jr.
Galveston, Texas

Big Red/Channel Bass Fishing

1

The Channel Bass

Its proper name is listed as the channel bass, but whether to call it this depends upon where one fishes. This fish, known to the marine biologist as *Sciaenops ocellatus,* is called the channel bass from Florida northward up the Atlantic Coast, but from the west side of Florida on around the Gulf Coast states and down into Mexico, it is the redfish. The Mexicans call it *pez colorado,* which translated is red fish.

Also labeled the red drum, bar bass, red bass, sea bass (erroneously), and surf bass, the fish is copper red with deeper red or brown spots on the scales that form the longitudinal stripe. It has a conspicuous black spot on the upper part of the tail base, and it is common for the fish to have two or three such spots. On adult fish these spots are about the size of a half dollar. Its lower sides are silvery gray with its belly shading to grayish-white. The fish has a reasonably streamlined body and a large head. Unlike many bottom feeders, it has no barbels on its chin. The outer teeth on the upper jaw are large.

The range of the channel bass is rather well defined with the extremes once extending from Massachusetts to the Yucatan. Since the turn of the century, its range has gradually decreased until now it is found only rarely in New York waters and only occasionally in waters from New York southward to Virginia. Its optimum range today is from Virginia southward through Mexico. Channel bass are found in the coastal waters from Tampico, Mexico, to the Yucatan, but sports anglers working these waters usually pass them up in favor of more highly prized gamefish such as tarpon and the large billfish.

The migration of channel bass has been the subject of much

study, and definite movements of the fish have been established. They move to deeper water in the late fall with the coming of cooler water and then move back inshore to shallower surf and bay waters in the spring as water temperatures rise. In hot weather they move into reasonably deep water and venture back into shallow water at night when temperatures cool.

They spawn in inlets and in the Gulf of Mexico, in inlets as well as the surf. The spawning usually takes place in September along the Atlantic Coast and in October in the Gulf Coast states.

Young channel bass spend the first year of their life in shallow and sheltered bay waters, or until they are about 12 to 13 inches long. Fish up to approximately 18 inches in length are called "puppy drum" along the Atlantic Coast and "rat reds" along the Gulf Coast. When the fish run in excess of 25 pounds, they are usually referred to as "bulls." Until the fish are three to four years old they return to bays and inlets, with the general movement being inshore in the spring and offshore in winter. After they reach maturity, they rarely move into bays and are found only in deep water except during the annual spring and fall runs in the surf.

The channel bass is one of several species of salt-water fish that come under conservation laws that apply to minimum length and bag limits as far as the sports fisherman is concerned. There are additional conservation laws protecting the fish when commercial fishing and netting are involved. For example, the minimum limit in Texas is 14 inches. Fish in excess of 35 inches, head on, are legal to catch by sportsmen but are illegal to sell. Since the fish don't spawn until they are three to four years old, the laws are designed to protect the large breeding fish and preserve the brood stock.

Within its normal range, the channel bass enjoys an exalted position, especially with surf casters. It is one of the sea's few big gamefish that requires little special or expensive fishing tackle. Consequently it falls within the taking of the budget-minded fisherman. A fellow with an economy $19.95 surf rig stands as much chance of getting a big channel bass as does the man with several hundred dollars worth of fishing gear and a plush fishing boat.

But while this fishing can be quite inexpensive, it is not easy.

What the fisherman may save in money by not having to buy special gear is cancelled out by one other factor: knowledge about the fish and its habits. Without this the fisherman can find channel bass fishing just as expensive as offshore charterboat billfishing if he places a monetary value on his time. The toughest obstacle to overcome is time. Once the fisherman learns to accept the fact that long hours—often unproductive ones—are necessary, he will find he has the battle more than half won.

The channel bass is a fish that can be caught on natural baits and artificial lures. Most, however, are caught on natural baits, live or dead, because the kind of water the fish prefers makes use of artificial lures difficult. Lures are most effective in clear water, and clear water is just the kind that redfish don't like.

Even though its range of plenty in the United States proper is restricted to nine states, plus occasional appearance in three others, the fish ranks 18th in annual take. In *The 1965 Salt-Water Angling Survey,* published by the Bureau of Sport Fisheries and Wildlife, U.S. Department of Interior, the channel bass take in the United States was placed at 11,200,000 fish. When the 18 species taken in the survey are divided into true gamefish and strictly food fish, the channel bass climbs up the ladder to eighth place. Many of the species that outnumbered the channel bass catch cover a far wider range, and in addition some of the species include sub-species.

The 18 species listed in the survey with the estimated take in parentheses (in millions) include:

1. Seatrouts	(89.4)	10. Atlantic mackerels	(22.8)
2. Flatfishes	(54.7)	11. Spot	(21.5)
3. Croakers	(51.1)	12. White perch	(20.2)
4. Puffers	(42.7)	13. Mullets	(18.5)
5. Catfishes	(41.7)	14. Striped bass	(18.5)
6. Porgies	(36.6)	15. Spanish mackerels	(17.9)
7. Snappers	(31.6)	16. Kingfishes	(13.1)
8. Bluefish	(30.5)	17. Bonitos	(13.0)
9. Grunts	(26.3)	18. Red drum	(11.2)

The species are listed exactly as they appear in the government publication, which can be purchased for 40 cents from The Superintendent of Documents, U.S. Government Printing Office, Washington, D.C. 20402. Note that the channel bass is referred to by

still a third name, "red drum," by the government. In sports
fishing circles, however, the names channel bass and redfish are
far more acceptable. There is a drum, the black drum, which
gets as large as a channel bass. The black drum, which makes
surf runs about the same time as the channel bass, is a poor
fighter sadly lacking in gamefish qualities. Of these 18 fish only
some of the seatrouts, flatfishes, bluefish, Atlantic mackerels,
striped bass, Spanish mackerels, bonitos, and channel bass are
true gamefish. The other species are not.

The channel bass is both a deep water and shoreline fish,
depending upon the time of the year. Consequently in those
states where they are plentiful, there are a great many places to
fish. Since the fish moves into shallow water in the surf and bays,
and small ones go as far as salt water moves up streams and
bayous, the fishing areas are quite extensive.

The tidal shorelines of the channel bass states range from a
low of 607 miles for Alabama to a high of 8,426 miles for Florida.
These tidal shoreline surveys were made in 1939-40 with a re-
cording instrument used on the largest scale charts and maps
then available. The survey covered the shoreline of outer coast,
offshore islands, sounds, bays, and up rivers and creeks to a point
where tidal waters narrowed to a width of 100 feet.

Following is the tidal shoreline in miles for the various channel
bass states: Florida (8,426), Louisiana (7,721), Texas (3,359),
North Carolina (3,375), Virginia (3,315), South Carolina (2,876),
Georgia (2,344), and Alabama (607).

The figures for the states where the channel bass used to roam
in numbers include: Maryland (3,190), New York (1,850), Delaware (381), and New Jersey (131).

A combination of pollution, destruction of tidal bay spawning
grounds, and shoreline urbanization is the reason for the decline
in movement of channel bass into waters of states north of
Virginia.

2
Where to Go

The best surf fishing for channel bass occurs in the spring and fall months with the run in the fall ranking well out front. Bay fishing for smaller fish generally ranges from spring through fall with the span becoming longer the more one travels southward to temperate waters.

This chapter will deal with the coast by states, from the Virginia coast on the Atlantic seaboard southward, down Florida and the loop through the Gulf Coast states, and down the eastern coast of Mexico. This is the optimum range of the channel bass. These fish are no longer plentiful along the coasts of New York, New Jersey, Delaware, and Maryland.

VIRGINIA

January and February are poor channel bass months in Virginia. The surf and bays will be empty of these fish, although when weather and seas permit a few big ones can be caught from boats in deep water. Stragglers begin to show up in the surf in March and this peaks into fair to good runs through April and May. A good many are also caught from boats in deep water during this period.

The surf fishing begins to slack off in June with the bays beginning to become the payoff spots for smaller channel bass. Bay fishing, which includes working the mouths of rivers and creeks on high tides, continues good through August.

Surf fishing becomes popular again in September with runs

far superior to those experienced in the spring months. The channel bass run in the surf reaches its peak in late September and then around mid-October begins to taper off. During this fall run as many large fish are caught from the piers as from the surf. November and December are poor months, although a few fish are taken from boats in deep water.

Virginia waters are the best choice for the fisherman interested in catching trophy fish. Channel bass caught there are consistently larger than those taken along any other coasts. The rod and reel world record channel bass of 83 pounds was caught from Virginia waters.

Some of the choice areas for channel bass in this state include Chesapeake Bay, Potomac River, Colonial Beach, bays and creeks around Hampton Roads, Virginia Beach, Chincoteague, Kiptopeke, Sand Bridge, Wash Woods, and False Cape.

NORTH AND SOUTH CAROLINA

In these two states January and February are poor months, although some channel bass can be taken in deep-water channels and a few big ones from offshore deep water. Even though most of the big fish are taken from boats, channel bass begin to appear in the surf in March with the run increasing in April and peaking in May. Also during May small fish are plentiful along the southern coast and in the bays.

The June through August period is a doldrum one. The few channel bass that are caught during this period are usually taken from deep water at night.

Small fish become plentiful again in September, which is also the start of the fall surf run. Most of the small fish are found in the bays and creeks. The surf run on big channel bass, fish almost comparable in size with those caught from Virginia waters, peaks in October and then begins to taper off after the middle of November. When December rolls around, the action is very slow again.

North Carolina has a number of famous channel bass areas including Outer Banks, Hatteras, Core Cape, Albemarle Sound,

Pamlico Sound, and the beaches from Morehead City south to Carolina Beach and Cape Fear.

South Carolina offers good redfish action in its surf from Little River Inlet to Folly Beach off Charleston. From Charleston south the state offers a coastline laced with rivers, creeks, and back water bays and sounds that offer fine fishing for small channel bass.

GEORGIA

Georgia's coast offers fair to good surf channel bass runs in April and May and again in September through the middle of November. The fall run is better than that in the spring. The June through August period offers good action for small channel bass in the mouths of the many rivers and creeks. Small ones can also be taken in deep channels and creeks in December, with January and February being the poorest fishing months. What hurts Georgia's reputation for channel bass fishing more than anything else is the lack of publicity on its coastal fishing. As a result the state attracts relatively few out-of-state fishermen.

FLORIDA

The upper Florida coast on the Atlantic side experiences the same seasons as those found in Georgia, but as one works southward, fishing for channel bass becomes more year around. Surf runs on the Florida Atlantic Coast are only fair, and this is probably due to the fact that the coast has become so urbanized and taken over by the bathers, surfers, and boaters.

From Miami on around the Keys and well back northward up the state's west coast, the action for channel bass is all year around. Large reds, which run considerably smaller than those taken on the Virginia coast, can be caught from deep water in the December through February period. The bays and tidal flats of this same area offer top flight fishing for small channel bass in the five- to 15-pound class from April through September. The shoals of Florida Bay and shallows in the Everglades National

Park region offer excellent action. As the weather cools, the larger fish move to deeper water but still within easy access of the fisherman.

As one works north up the west Florida coast and then westward across the Gulf Coast states, the fish is referred to as the redfish far more frequently than channel bass.

The coastal waters of the Florida panhandle are good almost the year around for fish up to about 15 pounds. Fishing along this section of the coast is poorest December through March. Fair to good surf redfish runs occur in October and November.

ALABAMA AND MISSISSIPPI

Good redfish action months for Alabama and Mississippi coincide. From January through February the fish are found in the surf around the offshore islands, which are quite numerous. Smaller redfish move in closer and come into the bays from April through July, and in August they move well up into the bays, creeks, and bayous.

September is the best month for fishing the surf. This surf fishing begins to taper off in October. Smaller fish move into inland deeps and rivers in November, while the large redfish are still fairly plentiful in the surf of the offshore islands through December.

Alabama has little coastline, and it is restricted to the Mobile Bay complex, Perdido Bay, and Dauphin Island.

Mississippi boasts many good redfish areas, some of which are Chandeleur, San Louis Bay, Breton Sound, Grand Gosier, Freemason Key, and the offshore islands of Cut, Ship, Horn, North, Deer, and Petit Bois.

LOUISIANA

Louisiana is the state where a fellow can catch redfish—not bulls, but two to five pounders—miles inland from the coast proper. The coast of Louisiana is a vast marsh that is often inundated by flood tides. Consequently redfish can be found far inland.

January through March is the time to fish the inland deeps and bayous for small redfish. When April comes, the fish move out of the inland deeps and channels into the shallow bays where they are abundant through June. Some bulls are taken from the surf in May, but in June through early September the big fish move to the deep water around the offshore islands.

Louisiana's surf run usually starts in late September, climbs to full peak in October, and begins to taper off in November with the fish moving back to deep water around offshore islands in December.

Prime areas for redfish in Louisiana include all the bayous and tidal bays of the Mississippi River delta, Lake Pontchartrain, Atchafalaya Bay, West Cote Blanche Bay, Vermillion Bay, Southwest Pass, Calcasieu Pass, Calcasieu Lake, and the offshore islands.

TEXAS

Texas boasts the longest and most accessible beaches of any state on the Gulf Coast. From Sabine Pass, where Texas joins Louisiana, then south to Brownsville, where the state meets Mexico, there stretches a complex of beaches approximately 700 miles long.

The poorest time for redfishing in Texas waters is in January and February, although a few large reds can be caught in offshore deep water and in deep ship channels. On the southern tip of the state where waters are warmer, small reds can be caught the year round.

The fish return to the bays and begin spreading out in March with good rat red fishing extending through May in the bays. A moderate run of bulls takes place in the surf in March but quickly tapers off in May as the large fish return to deep water. The June through August period is good for 10- to 20-pound fish in deep water and around jetties.

Bay fishing for rat reds begins to pick up again in late August and extends through November. Around mid-September the bulls return to the surf with the runs peaking in October and then tapering off in late November. In December rat reds are plentiful in inland deep holes, and a few bulls can be taken in deep offshore waters.

Texas beaches for surf fishing include Bolivar Peninsula, Galveston Island, Matagorda Peninsula, Matagorda Island, and Padre Island. Behind these beaches are expansive but shallow bays that offer excellent fishing for rat reds. These include the Galveston Bay complex, Matagorda Bay, Lavaca Bay, San Antonio Bay, Copano Bay, Corpus Christi Bay, and the 150-mile-long Laguna Madre. At times redfish also move well into the mouth of the Rio Grande River.

MEXICO (EAST COAST)

In Mexican waters the best surf runs occur in October and November. A few can also be taken from the surf in January and February. In December the fish congregate in good numbers near the mouths of rivers. Redfish are also plentiful around river mouths from March through June with the action beginning to taper off in July. August and September are dull months for redfish in Mexican waters, although some can be taken in deep water. The fish move back into the rivers and the surf in October.

Although Mexico has a lot of fishable coastline and coastal bays, relatively few sportsmen visit the area because of transportation difficulties, especially when it comes to driving to the coast from the interior. Highways are good to major cities and ports, but these are few and far between. The best way to reach the good but remote areas is to fly in, and even then it is advisable to get a guide.

The coastline of Mexico stretches 1,600 miles, but most of the sections are quite primitive. Good places to try for redfish include the lagoons, coves, inlets, and tide rips along the coast. Incidentally, many of these spots go unnamed on the map. Other good areas to try include Soto la Marina River, Panuco River, Tuxpan River, the coast north of Tampico, and the lagoons around the Tampico district.

3

When to Go

There is more to channel bass fishing than just picking the right time of the year. Although these fish can be caught day or night, the fellows who get the big ones consistently are those who fore-sake the late show on television.

The fisherman should always keep in mind that channel bass, whether they are large or small, are quite wary and tend to spook rather easily. They shy away from noisy areas and are extremely skitterish if the water is clear. When the water is gin clear, channel bass fishermen either stay home or console them-selves by seeking other varieties of fish. Channel bass fishing is best when the water is rough and sandy. Since the rough water noises will cover many noises made by the fishermen on the beach, the fish will often move in to within a few yards of the shoreline. These fish feed more by smell than sight, therefore clear water isn't necessary. This holds true for almost all species of fish that are bottom-feeders or feed by smell.

Bathers, surfers, and boaters often mess up surf action during the day because of the commotion they make. But at night, when these pleasure seekers vacate the area, the fish will move back near the shore. If the fisherman is averse to night fishing, he can compromise and do rather well by doing his fishing in a period from about two hours before sunrise until an hour or so after sunrise, before the beach frolickers make their appearance. Another good time to try is the early part of the evening after the pleasure seekers have left the water. For best results the fisherman going out early morning or evening must take tides into consideration. This aspect of channel bass fishing is fully covered in Chapter 4, Picking the Tides.

Night surf fishing is quite pleasant. In addition to the lack of manmade beach noises, the fisherman will find he has far less competition from other fishermen, more open areas to fish, and cooler air and water temperatures. Fish are much like people in that they move to areas where the surroundings are most comfortable. An additional advantage in night fishing is that the surf is far more alive with baitfish and small marine life. After the sun goes down, this small marine life comes out of hiding and forages in the shallow surf for food. This abundance of bait lures the big channel bass into shallow water for easy feeding.

Bay fishing for small channel bass is also best at night, around dawn and shortly after dusk. Small marine life in the bays is most active at night. Bay fishing in the middle of the day isn't much unless tides are flood, the water is cool, and there is a heavy overcast to hide the sun. This doesn't hold true if there are deep 20- and 30-foot holes in a bay, for when the sun begins to heat the surface of the water, the fish will move into these holes. The fisherman can find such bays on the Atlantic seaboard where the difference between high and low tides can be as much as six feet. Deep bays are uncommon along the Gulf Coast states where tide differences are likely to range only to an extreme of about two feet between high and low stands. Most of the deep holes found in Gulf Coast states' bays are those dredged out by man. Boat traffic keeps large numbers of fish from moving into these channels.

The daylight hours fisherman will have better luck with channel bass if he confines his fishing to piers and around jetties where the water is deep. I have caught many channel bass in the heat of an August sun in early afternoon fishing near jetties where the water was 30- to 40-feet deep. These same fish when night falls and waters cool will move toward shallower water, and in the fall they will move right into the surf where the water is only a few feet deep.

This doesn't mean that channel bass can't be caught in deep jetty waters at night. I have caught a good many this way, but night fishing off a jetty or from a boat nearby has its hazards and should not be attempted by a tyro.

Night fishing for channel bass can also be good from piers, and is far safer than venturing out on jetties. Most piers, especially those that charge a fee, have all the comforts to make night fishing pleasant and safe. The only drawback is the competition one gets from other anglers. There is always the problem of someone casting over your line and tangling up rigs. When a big fish is hooked, most fellow fishermen are sportsmen enough to reel in their lines to give you room to battle your fish. Unfortunately there are also a few hardheads around who need to be asked. Usually they will begrudgingly extend the courtesy at the last minute, but sometimes this last minute isn't soon enough.

Even if a section of beach is free of bathers, surfers, and boaters during the day, it won't be much day or night if one fishes at the wrong time of the year. Channel bass will not be in the surf in the dead of winter nor the heat of summer. The time to go is in the spring and fall, with the fall being the number one choice.

Blue northers that suddenly barrel across the Gulf Coast states and particularly in Texas and Louisiana make for some unusual winter fishing for small channel bass or rat reds. Texas and Louisiana bays are shallow and these blue northers that come howling in with 30- to 50-mile-an-hour winds "blow the water out of the bays." These winds cause water levels to drop far below normal and often expose miles of sand and mud flats. The fish naturally move to deep water. The accompanying 20- to 30-degree temperature drop chills surface waters, which causes the rat reds to school in great masses in deep holes.

When fishermen find these holes at the right time, they can get into some mighty sporty action. The fish will be right on the bottom, and the fisherman can catch them by the dozens if he knows the technique to use. Live shrimp make the best bait, but unfortunately in the winter live shrimp can be scarce at bait camps. The fisherman can then either use small bits of cut mullet or whole dead shrimp if he prefers to fish natural baits. If he elects to go with artificial lures, the best choices are red and white or yellow bottom-bumping plugs, silver spoons with either a red or yellow bucktail or yellow, red, or white worm-jigs. The worm-jig is simply a leadhead jig with a plastic worm slipped over the shank of the hook.

Whether live bait, dead bait, or artificial lures is used, the style of fishing must be slow. Jig and hippity-hop the bait or lure slowly along the bottom. Normally rat reds strike with a jolt in warm weather, a jolt hard enough to set the hook. In real cold water, however, the rats pick up and mouth the bait much like the big bulls in the surf. Consequently the fisherman must be alert when the fish picks up the bait, and he must strike to set the hook. The bites are a lot like those of bait-stealing piggies and small catfish that so often plague the fisherman when the water is warm.

I have seen some really wild rat red catches made from deep holes in frigid weather. One such run took place in the Crash Boat Basin at Galveston, Texas, back in the early 1950s. The fish schooled in a deep hole at the far end of the basin. Fishermen were 10 to 15 feet apart and lined the bank for about 200 yards. The temperature was down around 25 degrees, and although salt water won't freeze until it drops to 16 degrees or below, conditions were such that moisture in the air immediately above the surface condensed and froze to form skim ice on the surface. Neither live nor dead bait was available at the time, so all the fishermen were using artificials, most of which were spoons. All the fish caught were quite uniform in size, running around one and a half to two pounds. Catches ranged from a half dozen to three dozen fish per man. I was fortunate enough to be fishing at the time, and I landed 16. Newspaper accounts written about the run estimated that approximately 5,000 fish were taken that morning.

It was a lot of fun but catches like that convince me that a bag limit should be placed on the fish. A fisherman should be allowed to catch them as long as they are around, but there should be a limit as to how many fish he can keep. It would be a good conservation measure toward protecting brood stock of the future.

4

Picking the Tides

Although it is quite true that channel bass can be taken on any tide, there are certain ones that offer better fishing than others. Going fishing on the high tide is no guarantee for catching channel bass, even though it would be a better choice than going out on the low tide.

The changing of tides from high to low and back again is a slow process. Through the course of a year, tide changes and heights of respective high and low tides will vary. Along some coasts the number of tides during a 24-hour period can range from one to four. An area can have one high or low tide in the period but no corresponding opposite tide. There can be two tides—a high and a low—or three tides—two highs and a low or vice versa. On days with four tides there will be two highs and two lows.

Take the situation of four daily tides. Don't bet any money the tide stands will be about six hours apart or even evenly spaced. There will be four-tide days when the period between a high and a low, or vice versa, can be as short as two hours. The fisherman must likewise note the difference in water height between the high and low stands. Within the range of the channel bass on our coasts this variation can be from as little as a foot on up to six feet. The difference under normal weather conditions on the Atlantic Coast can be as much as six feet. The normal difference along the Gulf Coast states is one and a half to two feet, while down the Mexican coast it ranges from a foot to a foot and a half.

If this fish ranged as far north as Argentia, Newfoundland, the coastal tide variation would go up to around nine feet. If the channel bass ranged as far south in South America as Punta Loyola, Argentina, the difference between high and low tides could range more than 40 feet within a 24-hour period. Just imagine the force of tides and currents in the Punta Loyola area for May 1, 1968. Tide tables for that date listed a low tide of 0.4 feet at 4:57 A.M. At 10:48 A.M. the same date the incoming tide reached a high stand of 40.1 feet. Then at 5:25 P.M. the next low was down to −0.6 feet, with the following high at 11:09 P.M. up to 40.7 feet. Fortunately we don't have to fight tides like this within the channel bass range in North American waters.

The man who knows his channel bass fishing pays close attention to the tides. He can get the information on a day to day basis from his daily newspaper, radio, or television. Along the coasts I don't know of a single daily newspaper that does not carry this information, either in a weather box on the front page or in a fishing column in the sports section. Some papers like *The Galveston Daily News,* on which I work, list tide information both on page one and in the sports section. Every Friday morning I run a box on the sports page listing the tides for the next seven days. Fishermen tell me it is invaluable in enabling them to plan ahead.

The fellow who fishes in a number of areas will find it to his advantage to purchase annually a copy of the U.S. Coast and Geodetic Survey's *Tide Tables, East Coast of North and South America Edition.* It is available in a number of coastal book stores, marine supply houses, and yacht basins, or it can be ordered from the U.S. Government Printing Office, Washington, D. C., 20402. The current price is two dollars, but I doubt if real fishermen would complain if the price was ten because the book is a gold mine of information that can be correlated into successful fishing.

The Coast and Geodetic Survey has published *Tide Tables* for the use of mariners since 1853. The *East Coast of North and South America Edition* lists full daily predictions for 48 reference stations and the differences for approximately 2,000 stations in North and South America. In addition it contains a table for obtaining the approximate height of the tide at any time; a table of local mean time of sunrise and sunset for every fifth day of the year for different latitudes; a table for the reduction of local mean time to standard time, moonrise, and moonset for eight places; and a table of Greenwich mean time of the moon's phases, apogee, perigee, greatest north and south and zero declination, and the time of the solar equinoxes and solstices.

All this information, while it is of prime importance to the mariner, can also be used by the fisherman, especially those who fish the surf and bays where tidal actions have great influence on fish. High and low tides are of little consequence to fishing when it is done far offshore in deep water.

The *Tide Table* lists tide stands according to the 24-hour clock. Midnight is listed as 00:00. The time goes one through 12 for A.M., and 13 through 23 for P.M. For example 1 P.M. will appear in the book as 13:00. The time 11:59 A.M. will appear as 11:59, but 11:59 P.M. will be listed as 23:59. The times are standard for the part of the coast covered. If Daylight Savings Time is employed, then an hour must be added to each of the times listed in the book. This can cause the tide to "flop" to the succeeding day. For example, a 23:30 tide stand will flop to 00:30 when Daylight Savings Time is used.

Tides are based on moon rise and set and the various phases of the moon. Tides rise as the moon rises, and they fall as the moon declines. How strong or weak a tide may be depends upon the pull exerted during various lunar phases. Tides are strongest during the full phase and weakest during the first and last quarters. Tides run highest in the summer and lowest in the winter.

The time predictions for the high and low tides are exact. Predictions on the height of the water at either high or low would be exact if dead-calm weather conditions existed 24 hours a day for 365 days a year. The dead-calm is rare, so height conditions can show considerable differences between predicted and actual water heights on a given high or low stand. Sustained offshore winds will keep a high tide from reaching its predicted height and make a low tide fall lower. It is vice versa on a sustained onshore wind. The stronger the wind, the greater the variation. The barometer also comes into play on water heights. The higher the barometer, the lower the tide.

A fisherman, whether he fishes the surf, the jetties or the bays, should know the meaning of various terms applied to tides. The terms with their meanings are as follows:

FLOODING—When the tide is coming in.

HALF TIDE—The midway point between flooding and peak high; also the midway point between peak high and extreme low.

HIGH WATER SLACK—When the water reaches its peak on the high tide phase.

FLOOD TIDE—Same as high water slack.

DIURNAL—When high water has an approximate stand of seven hours.

EBBING—When tide ends its high stand and begins to fall.

LOW WATER SLACK—Low tide at its lowest point.

TURN OF THE TIDE—The change from one tide to the other.

DEAD WATER—This occurs on both high and low water slacks when the current stops.

MEAN TIDE—The average water height over a year period between high and low water slacks.

Other terms like "high," "low," "incoming," and "outgoing" are perfectly acceptable to use, and throughout this book frequent references to tides will be made in these general terms.

This tide parlance is to the veteran fisherman what "port" and "starboard" are to the boatman. A poor fellow who invades yachting circles and starts talking about the left or right side of a boat is likely to be tossed into the drink.

Now to correlate the tides with fishing. Slack water, whether high or low, and dead water are poor times to go fishing as small baitfish tend to scatter and can more easily escape larger fish. High slack, however, can be good in bay fishing, especially when the water is at such heights to flood salt grass flats. This is the time to go after those small channel bass.

Either high or low slack have relatively little bearing on jetty fishing if the surrounding waters are deep. On low slack the fish will tend to gather in the deep holes, but they will fan out on high slack. However, because of the abundance of marine life around the rocks, the fish are likely to work in close proximity to the jetties. You can catch channel bass on dead water at the jetties, but the action will be far slower than that at either high or low slacks.

Tides play a most important part in surf fishing, and with channel bass particularly so at night, dawn, and dusk. Usually the fishing is best during the first two hours of flooding and the first two hours of ebbing.

When the tide begins to flood, or start in, the channel bass will begin to move in toward the beaches to feed. If the fisherman happens to be out during the normal spring and fall runs, he will often find the fishing good through the entire flooding stage and even on high water if the dead water period is of short duration. Low water slack, a time when sand bars normally covered with water bleach white in the sun, is the worst possible time to seek channel bass in the surf. Those that are caught during this period are usually taken from piers that extend well out into deep water. Even then the action is certain to be slow.

If the fisherman decides to use the surf chum box described in the chapter on Special Tricks, he should do so on the flood or ebb tide stages when there are moving currents. The surf chum box is useless during the dead water period since there is no current to fan out the chum to make a slick. Use of this box is almost as bad on fast changing tides, for the currents may be so swift as to swirl chum up near the surface and above the bottom-feeding channel bass.

5
Rods, Reels, and Lines

My earliest recollection of surf tackle was the gear my father and his friends used back in the Depression years. The reels were outlandishly large. Some had drag devices but most were knuckle-busters with only leather thumb stalls to provide the drag. The more drag pressure one needed to handle a running fish, the more the fisherman pressed down on the leather tab that rested against the reel spool. It was common to wet the leather to keep one's thumb from being burned by the heat generated by the line as it was stripped off by a big fish.

The line itself was linen of 50 or more pounds test. And the rods. They were something to behold. Most all were homemade affairs out of calcutta cane. Guides were wrapped on with fishing line, and fishing line no longer good enough to hold the big fish was wrapped around the rod handle from reel seat to butt. This in turn was shellacked and varnished to keep the windings sealed and protected from rot. Reel seats were simple metal clamps, usually homemade, too.

The rods, which varied in length from 9 to 14 feet, all had one thing in common—a permanent set or bend. Repeated casting of heavy sinkers and fishing big fish put the bends in the rods. There was no such thing as a straight rod. My dad and his fishing buddies tried to beat the bend by storing the rods with weights attached to the tips so the bend would be in the opposite direc-tion. The rods straightened out, but only until the next fishing trip. And then there was that same old set again. The rods looked both ungainly and unbeautiful. But, man, how they got the job done.

Those rods had whip in them. They would bend almost U-shape when a fellow made his cast. But there was that whip that fired the terminal tackle seaward like a shot. It enabled a fellow to make long casts with ease. This was important from a standpoint of other than getting the bait far out to sea. All this took place in the days when there just wasn't spare money around to buy chest high waders, and the October and November surfs were far too cold to wade out in waist-deep to make a cast. A fellow with hip boots was indeed a lucky soul. Most of them had to settle for knee boots, and this meant one never waded out more than a few steps from the shoreline.

And then after each fishing trip there was that tiresome chore of spooling all the linen line off the reel, washing it in fresh water, and then stretching it out to dry. If you didn't do this, the line would rot quickly.

Tackle today is far more sophisticated. We still have some calcutta rods around, homemade affairs by fellows who built them to suit their own personal tastes. Some are beautiful pieces of workmanship, but no matter how much care goes into the building and upkeep, they still have that set. My dad used to say of his old rods that the set gave them "character" and the look of having caught big fish. I think he had something there because I hear today's youngsters, who never went through the calcutta age, see a fellow walking down the beach with a calcutta rod and its inevitable set and remark: "That fellow must have caught a big one to put a bend like that in his rod."

Today surf rods are built of glass and are far superior to the old calcutta sticks. To begin with they won't take a set. They have a lot of whip much more uniform than the old calcuttas and will permit for much longer casts. They are strong and have the backbone to handle big fish. The uniform whip in their tips provides a much better shock absorber than calcutta did when a fish made a sudden run.

Rods today come in all lengths and in light, medium, and heavy action. The rod length and action for channel bass angling will be determined by where you fish. The surf calls for an entirely different kind of rod than those used from boats, piers, or around jetties. Then back in the bays there is still another type of rod to use.

Good surf rods range from 7 to 14 feet in length. This length is necessary to get the needed power to make long casts. The length of the tip is what gives the whip when pressure is applied in casting. A short, stiff tip will not permit long casts in the true sense of casting. You can get fair distance with the stout stick, but you can do so only by heaving or swinging the terminal tackle out.

The length of the surf rod, whether it is a 7- or 14-foot model, includes both tip and handle. A 14-inch handle is adequate for the 7-foot rod, but longer handles are needed with the longer tips. The 18-inch handle is right for rods up to 12 feet in length, and the really long rods require a 24-inch handle. The handle length is important in order to get leverage to cast.

The beginning fisherman should not go off half cocked and buy the longest rod he can find on the assumption that it will enable him to cast a country mile. He should try casting with rods of various lengths to learn what is best suited for his casting style and ability. A big fellow with excellent coordination can handle the long rod. A little five-foot-six fellow with the same coordination is likely to discover that the 7 to 9 footer is his cup of tea. I'm five-nine and I can handle surf rods up to 12 feet in length. My casts with longer ones are botchy.

Care must be taken in matching the rod to the reel. A spinning reel on a rod designed for the conventional revolving spool reel is a bad mismatch that will penalize the fisherman on distance in casting. The conventional reel fitted on a spinning rod is even worse.

BOAT, PIER, AND JETTY RODS

Rods used for channel bass when fishing the jetties or from boats and piers are shorter and stouter than those used in the surf. These rods usually range from 6 to 8 feet in length. They lack the sharp whip of the surf rod since distance casting is not necessary. The rod tip, however, should be limber enough to

A pair of scrappy channel bass caught from the Louisiana surf. Called redfish in Louisiana, these fish offer fine action in surf runs in fall months. Note distinctive black spot markings on the tails of the fish. Occasionally these fish may have black spots along lateral line on body. (Photo courtesy Louisiana Tourist Development Commission)

Two fine channel bass caught in a night of fishing from a pier. Red-fish often move into very shallow water at night.

This shell-encrusted part of a tree is a **curio** as far as sightseers are concerned. It is also a key to shell life offshore. Channel bass like to feed on the small shell life clustered on the tree.

This mass of shell on water's edge is a clear indication that nearby waters are rich with fodder for bottom-feeding fish such as the redfish.

Redfish often ingest whole shells when they are feeding. This photo is of a mass of actual-size shells recovered from the stomachs of two freshly caught 30-pound redfish.

This Penn Peerless No. 9 reel is an ideal all around reel for bay, surf, and jetty fishing for redfish.

Open-face spinning reels like this Mitchell 402 are ideal for making long casts in fishing the surf.

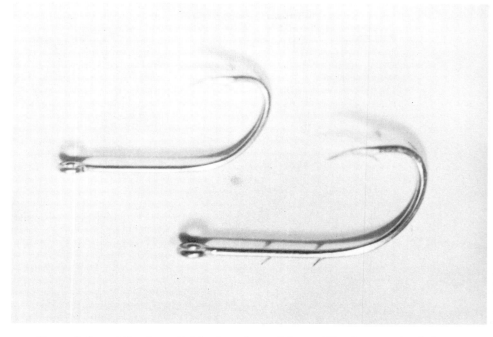

Two styles of hooks suitable for channel bass. The bottom hook has barbs on its shank to hold soft baits in place.

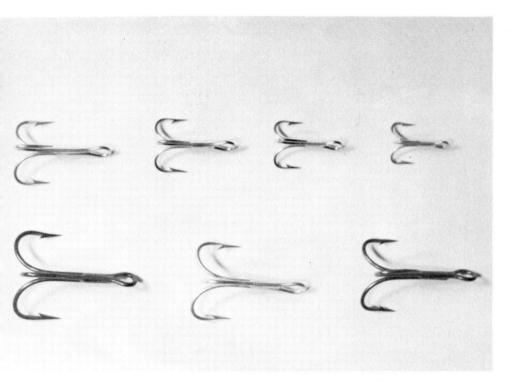

These are actual-size treble hooks for small redfish. Smallest hooks can be completely imbedded in the bait. These hooks are light enough so as not to impede action when live baits are used.

Line connector is handy to connect leader to line. It can also be used to make up fish-finder rig.

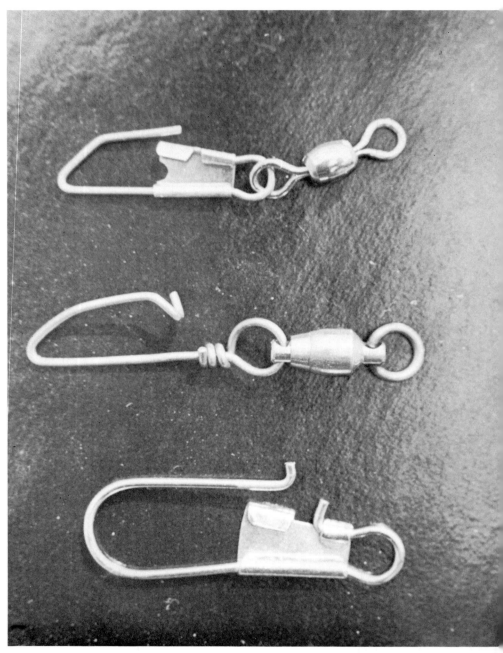

Snaps and swivels rigged to hooks can prevent line twist. The extra weight of this hardware, however, can limit action when small live baits are used. When big fish are involved, use snaps that lock such as the center and bottom ones pictured.

This angler is cutting a small fish into chunks for redfish bait. This bait will stay on the hook and won't be bothered by small trash fish.

Dead shrimp make good channel bass bait, but this is what is likely to happen if trash fish are around. The angler can spend the day catching catfish only slightly larger than the bait itself.

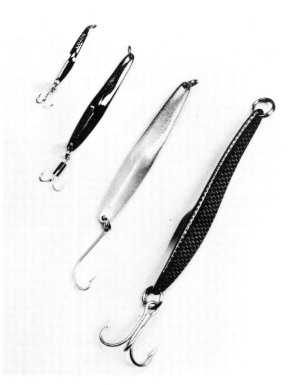

Four sizes of lucky lujon spoons that are suitable for channel bass fishing. The small models are fine for rat reds. The larger models have weight and shape for distance surf casting. (Photo courtesy Louis Johnson Co.)

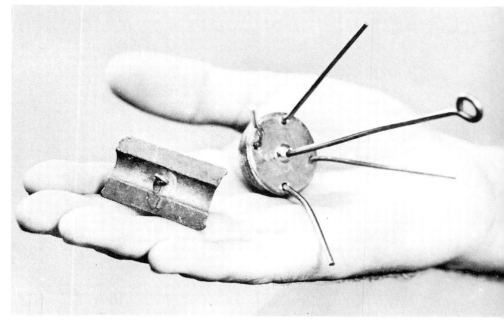

Two excellent sinkers for surf fishing. The model at the left is called Updegrove and the one on the right is Surf Sinker. Both have excellent holding ability in heavy surf.

provide a good shock absorber when the fish strikes or makes a sudden run.

The best rods are the hollow glass models. Since they are lighter in weight than solid glass, they are less tiring to use. Pier rods can be either hollow or solid. If no landing nets or long-handled gaffs are available on the pier, then the solid glass rod is the best choice since some catches may have to be lifted from the water to the pier decking.

Again the rods should be matched to the types of reels used. Cross-breeding of conventional rods with spinning reels, or vice versa, will result in a "cur" rig.

BAY RODS

Bay rods are lightweight and usually run 6 to 8 feet in length. Their action is a miniature of the surf rod. The whippy tip is necessary to make casting light baits and lures easy. This same whip is needed to cushion shocks so hooks will not be torn out of the flesh of the fish. Always keep in mind that the mouth of the small channel bass is much tenderer than that of the big bull.

These rods are available with 12- to 14-inch two-hand grips as well as the one-hand or semi-pistol grips. The type of handle is a matter of individual preference. Personally I prefer the two-hand grip since it provides extra leverage when having to cast into the wind and when battling a good size fish. Furthermore I find it less tiring to use when fishing long periods.

SURF REELS

Back in my father's redfishing days there were two types of reels: the conventional revolving spool reel and the fly reel. No one in Texas used the fly reel for redfish. In fact, in those days no saltwater fisherman would consider using a fly reel under any circumstances.

Today we have four types of reels: conventional, fly, spinning, and spin-cast. I will pass over the fly reel since this is used for a specialized kind of fishing and not more than a handful of fishermen use fly tackle for channel bass. Before the army of flyrodders gets ready to unload their arrows at me, let me hasten to point out that I do a lot of fly rod fishing in both salt and fresh water. I just don't use fly tackle for channel bass.

When it comes to surf fishing, the best reels are the conventional spool and open-face spinning models. The closed-face spin-cast reel is all right if a fellow wants to put up with frequent on-the-spot cleanings. The monofilament line used will pick up salt and sand in surf fishing, and closed face spin-cast reels have a bad habit of collecting this stuff under their hoods or cowls.

The surf reel must be large enough to carry 250 yards of line in the pound test you prefer to use. If your reel happens to have the capacity to spool on 400 yards of line, don't wind on just 250 yards and stop. Whether a reel is conventional, open-face spinning, or spin-cast, it will function better on the cast when the spool is full than when it is half-full.

Regardless of the type of reel used for the surf, it must have a smooth-functioning drag, which must be checked after each trip to make sure it is free of salt and sand deposits. Regardless of what type of fishing reel is used, it should be washed and dried before storage. And never store a reel with the drag screwed down tight. Over a long storage period this will press the drag washers and disks out of shape and cause the device to chatter or malfunction. It is no fun battling a big fish with a reel that has a drag chattering like a machine gun.

The open-face spinning reel has several distinct advantages in surf fishing. Since line peels off the spool easier, longer casts are possible. The backlash that is common with the conventional reel is eliminated with the spinning reel. The spinning reel also offers the advantage of permitting the use of lighter, finer diameter line.

The conventional reel has a marked advantage when it comes to fighting the fish. Its drag is easier to reach and much more controllable. But unless a fellow has a well-educated thumb, backlashes can become headaches.

BOAT, JETTY, PIER REELS

The identical reels the fisherman uses for surf fishing can be used around jetties or from boats and piers. Just make sure they are matched to the proper type rods.

The closed-face spin-cast reel is acceptable for this type of fishing since the fisherman won't have to contend with beach sand.

BAY REELS

Back in the bays is where one can go to the lightweight reels. The baitcasting, spinning, and spin-cast reels are excellent for this phase of channel bass fishing, but whatever type is used, the reel should have a smooth-working drag.

If the fisherman decides to go with the conventional baitcasting reel, be sure it is one with a level wind device. Remember in bay fishing you will be casting repeatedly and it can get mighty tiring thumbing line on the spool on each retrieve. I must point out that a lot of conventional spool reels suitable for surf, jetty, boat, and pier fishing are now available with level wind devices. The difference of a few bucks in the price is well worth the convenience.

LINES

When my father did his redfishing, linen line known as Cuttyhunk was the style for the surf, jetties, boats, and piers, while silk line was the vogue for bay fishing. Both lines were prone to rotting quickly unless they were given frequent washings and loving care.

A few fishermen today still use Cuttyhunk. The other 99 percent use synthetic lines—braided or monofilament. There is as much difference between linen line and the synthetics as there is between propeller-driven and jet planes.

The advantages of the synthetics are legion. To mention just a few, they are more uniform in strength, they have sufficient elasticity to absorb shock, they lose less test strength at point of knot, and they are practically deterioration proof. Like everything else there are good brands and cheap brands. The cheap synthetics are stiff, take a coil-like wire, and are subject to becoming brittle with age. Good synthetic line will last indefinitely. I have one surf reel that has gone through five seasons of hard fishing with the same line—and the line is still good.

When it comes to line strength, those testing 10 to 12 pounds are entirely adequate for bay fishing. Anything heavier on the lightweight reel will make for difficult casting.

For surf, jetty, boat, and pier fishing along the Gulf Coast, line testing 20 to 30 pounds is sufficient. If the fisherman prefers trolling, then he should go to the 40- to 50-pound test line. Fishermen along the Atlantic seaboard, particularly those fishing the surf, jetties, and piers along the coasts of Virginia and the Carolinas, should go to the 30- to 50-pound test line since the channel bass caught in this section are far larger than those normally taken on the Gulf Coast. The line can be correspondingly lighter test if a spinning reel and long, whippy spinning rod are used.

Just because the fish running may be 40 pounders, this doesn't mean that at least 40-pound test line is necessary. It would be if the fish had to be lifted deadweight. Frankly, if this was attempted with a 40-pound channel bass, the odds would be beautiful that the weight of the fish alone would cause the hook to tear out of its mouth.

When a fish is pulling on the line, it may seem like a tremendous pull. Actually it is likely to be less than half the weight of the fish involved. When the fish does make a run and exert a strain in excess of the line test, the line will hold as long as the rod has a whippy tip to absorb the initial shock and the reel drag is set light enough to allow the fish to strip off line.

If the rod is as unbending as a dockside boom and the drag is screwed tight, the line will snap at a sudden jerk if slack is allowed in the line. For example, a 20-pound test line will support a 20-pound weight without snapping. The same line will snap if a five-pound weight is tied to it and then dropped from the ceiling. The weight plus the momentum of the falling object in this case totals far in excess of the line test strength. If the fisherman has a lot of slack in his line and a 10-pound channel bass suddenly heads seaward full bore, the line will snap if there is no whippy rod tip and correctly set drag to cushion the shock.

All lines for a given test strength are not of the same diameter. This diameter doesn't become a factor until one fishes the surf. It takes less sinker weight to hold a fine diameter line out to sea than it does with a line of coarse diameter. The greater the line diameter the more likely the line will be rolled back to the beach by breaking waves and lateral currents.

I conducted some experiments with three lines: 50-pound test linen, 40-pound test monofilament, and 20-pound test mono-filament. All tests were made at the same time with identical rods and reels. It required eight ounces of lead to keep the linen line in place, five ounces to hold the 40-pound test mono-filament, and just three ounces to keep the 20-pound test mono-filament out to sea. Then I made tests with three 20-pound test monofilament lines of different diameter. The thickest line required four ounces of lead, the next needed three and a half ounces, while the line with the finest diameter was held in place with three ounces.

The difference between four and three ounces may be only a single ounce, but that one ounce can get to feel like a pound in long hours of casting into the surf.

6
Hooks and Leaders

The business end of a sports fishing rig, regardless of the species of fish sought, is the hook. This bit of bent steel that sells anywhere from a nickel up to several dollars is what latches the fish to the fisherman. Fishing for channel bass doesn't call for any highly specialized hooks, so the fisherman can forget all about the mention of two dollar hooks. These are used only in ultra specialized phases of some types of expensive offshore fishing. The hooks the channel bass fisherman will need range from the nickel to the 25 cent varieties.

Surf, jetty, and pier fishing call for one type of hook. An entirely different type is used when channel bass are sought in the bays. In addition to different types, there is also the matter of sizes.

Hooks must be big enough and strong enough to hold the species of fish sought, yet at the same time they must be small enough so that the fish doesn't have to open its mouth dental-chair wide in order to get it in. Many fishermen go on the assumption that the bigger the fish, the bigger the hook necessary. This is certainly true, but only up to a point. Other and more important factors concern the normal manner in which the channel bass feeds and the size of its mouth.

By way of comparison consider the 50-pound shark in relation to the 50-pound channel bass. Sharks normally feed in a slashing manner by opening their jaws wide and taking a mighty bite. This fish will take in a single gulp a two-pound chunk of bait imbedded on a six-inch hook that in turn is attached to a chain leader. The mouth of the 50-pound channel bass, however, is not nearly as large. Channel bass will occasionally slash at baits, too, but the baits will be far smaller than those taken by the shark. A foot-long mullet is a big bait for a 50-pound channel bass. The hook used with this bait should be not more than three inches in length from eye to bend. Hooks in the 3/0 to 9/0 range are of adequate size. Always keep in mind that the channel bass is a bottom-feeder that moves along leisurely picking up small food morsels off the bottom. Its habit is one of nosing and lipping baits before ingesting.

The fisherman who doubts this should spend some time watching channel bass feed in marine oceanariums. They work along close to the bottom, nosing and picking up chunks of food about half the size of a package of cigarettes. This fish, which feeds more by smell than sight, often noses a chunk of food for some time before picking it up. The only times I have observed them feeding recklessly was when several other channel bass moved in on the same chunk of food. Then the spirit of competition made them act in a hurry. Although even then the fish didn't open their mouths to the maximum. They opened just wide enough to ingest the chunks, and if there had been large hooks attached to the chunks, I doubt if they would ever have been taken in.

Quite frankly I feel that a lot of channel bass strikes that are missed are the result of fish clamping down on a portion of the bait and pulling it off the hook without the hook ever entering the fish's mouth.

When tyros consider the world record channel bass, an 83-pounder caught in Virginia waters, and the usual run of 30- to 40-pounders taken from the surf and around jetties and piers, they visualize using block and tackle-size hooks.

Again, the proper hook for surf, jetty, and pier fishing should never exceed three inches in length from eye to bend, and it should be a regular shank—not long-shank—model. My preference is a 3/0 Eagle Claw O'Shaughnessy ringed eye forged hook. This hook will hold channel bass caught in Texas waters, where I do the bulk of my fishing. If I fished the waters of Virginia and the Carolinas, I would go to 6/0 to 9/0 sizes. These hooks are small enough to be completely covered if one desires to use dead or cut bait. If live bait is used, the hooks are still small enough so as not to impede the swimming action of the bait. These hooks, properly bedded in the flesh of a fish's mouth, will handle a 100-pound fish. So why use huge hooks capable of holding 300 pounds of fish when the channel bass world record is only 83 pounds?

Use forged steel hooks, for they are difficult to bend. The hooks should have normal length straight shanks. If soft dead bait is used, it pays to use hooks that have slices on their shanks since they will hold the bait more securely in place. These are called "bait-holder" hooks.

When dead or cut bait is used, the bait should completely cover the hook with just the hook's point and barb exposed. If baitfish are cut up for bait, bones should be removed, for bone within a chunk of bait is likely to prevent the hook's point and barb from extending out enough to penetrate into the flesh of the fish's mouth.

Needless to say hooks should be honed razor sharp in order to gain maximum penetration without difficulty. In order to hold a big channel bass, it is necessary for the hook to penetrate to its bend. If penetration is only barb-deep, the hook will likely tear out of the flesh when the fish makes a sudden run. Should the barb-deep penetration be in a bony part of the fish's mouth, a sudden run could either bend the hook or outright break off the point and barb. Either way this means a lost fish. Forged hooks, however, are quite hard to either bend or break.

There is a time when a springy wire hook has an advantage over the forged one. This is when the fisherman is working an area with a lot of rocks and snags. When forged hooks foul in a snag, it means a broken line or leader. Either way it usually means loss of the entire terminal rig—hooks, leader, and sinker. And then one has to consider all the time lost in having to completely re-rig terminal gear. The springy steel wire hook will bend, even straighten out, and the fisherman can retrieve the entire terminal rig. It means, of course, putting on a new hook, but this is less trouble and time-consuming than having to make up an entirely new terminal rig.

The spring steel wire hook will hold a big channel bass if the fisherman plays the fish properly. With forged hooks a fisherman can do a lot of "horsing" with the fish; if wire hooks are used the "horsing" must be left out.

Some fishermen use treble or gang hooks in surf, jetty, and pier angling. They go on the assumption that three tines on a hook makes the odds three times better in their favor of hooking the fish. This undoubtedly is true to some extent, but look what happens after a big channel bass is hooked on a treble hook. Unless you can find forged treble hooks, which happen to be expensive, odds are good that a big channel bass will snap off one, perhaps all three, tines. The garden variety of treble hooks available in most tackle shops are soldered creations of easy-to-bend wire. It doesn't take much to either bend or break them. Where there is a good chance of getting into fish running in excess of 20 pounds, stay away from the treble hooks. Not only that, if you catch a channel bass that exceeds the existing world record by just a single ounce, your catch won't stand up as a new record. The International Game Fishing Association doesn't recognize as records any catches made on treble or gang hooks.

Treble hooks, however, do have their place in channel bass fishing. These are the ideal hooks to use when seeking small ones ranging up about five or six pounds.

At the outside the largest hook for bay fishing is the 5/0, with hooks in the 1/0 to 3/0 sizes being more ideally suited. These are the recommended sizes for single hooks. When it comes to treble hooks, the extra tines mean extra weight, which could hamper the action of live bait if the bait is quite small. Adequate sizes in treble hooks are numbers 1, 2, 4, or 6. If the fish run one to two pounds in size, the No. 6 hook is the best.

The hook measuring system originated in England. Hooks from No. 22 to 3 increase 1/16 inch in length as the size number decreases. From No. 3 up to 5/0 hooks become 1/8 inch longer with each size. From 5/0 on up to 20/0 the size increases in half-inch jumps. Unfortunately U.S. hook manufacturers follow little uniformity when it comes to the British sizing system. The majority of U.S. hooks have a standard length for a particular size, but U.S. makers also put out hooks with extra long or short shanks.

Deviations from regular sizes are indicated by X and the words "long" or "short." For example, a 2/0xL or 2/xLong designation means it is a 2/0 hook with a shank as long as the standard shank length of the next size larger hook, counting the odd as well as the even sizes. The normal 2/0 hook is 1-5/8 inches. The 2/0xL has a shank equal to the length of the 4/0 standard shank, which is 1 7/8 inches. On shortness of hook shanks the system reverses. A 2/0xS or 2/0xShort hook will have the length of a shank two sizes smaller. So instead of 1-5/8 inches it would have a 1-3/8 inch shank.

Hook Size Chart

Hook number	Length in inches	Hook number	Length in inches
20	5/32	2/0	1 5/8
18	7/32	3/0	1 3/4
16	9/32	4/0	1 7/8
14	11/32	5/0	2
12	7/16	6/0	2 1/2
10	9/16	7/0	3
8	11/16	8/0	3 1/2
6	13/16	9/0	4
4	15/16	10/0	4 1/2
3	1 inch	12/0	5
2	1 1/8	14/0	5 1/2
1	1 1/4	16/0	6
0	1 3/8	18/0	6 1/2
1/0	1 1/2	20/0	7

Hooks are measured from the bottom of the bend to the top of the shank, eye not included.

Cadmium and nickel-plated hooks are the best for salt-water use. Tinned hooks will also do for salt water, although the plating will eventually wear off. Other hook finishes such as gold-plated, silver-plated, blued, bronzed (brown lacquer), and japanned (black lacquer) are good for one salt-water fishing trip and that is all, for they either rust or corrode very easily. Use these hooks once and then throw them away.

There is no such thing as the all-purpose hook pattern. Various patterns are designed for various purposes and often specific species of fish. Recommended patterns for channel bass fishing include O'Shaughnessy, Eagle Claw, or Beak, Siwash, and Sproat.

Small channel bass have only a faint ridge of teeth that are not sharp at all. On channel bass under 20 pounds no wire leader is necessary. Instead use a good monofilament leader. Back in the bays and when live bait is used, the fisherman must use the finest monofilament leader possible, as a coarse leader will hamper the action of the bait. The monofilament leaders used for fish in excess of 20 pounds should be 40- to 60-pound test material. It is far more supple than even braided wire and it will allow the bait to swing freely in the current.

It is sometimes advisable to use wire leaders with large channel bass. They should certainly be used when trolling is involved. The teeth on large channel bass are dull. The ridges and edges of the fish's mouth are hard, and in a long fight, especially in rough water, a monofilament leader rubbing constantly against these edges can chafe in two. Wire leaders must be used around rocks. Here a hooked fish swimming alongside a barnacle-covered rock can chafe and break a monofilament leader in short order.

Back in the days when my father fished for redfish, the leader style was piano wire. It was stiff and springy and kept the bait from swinging naturally in the current. Today we have braided wire leaders that are far more supple and are covered with plastic, which helps to make them less visible to the fish and to protect the leader wire proper from rust and corrosion. Life of these leaders is much longer than that of the old piano wire models.

Most channel bass leaders, even when live bait is used, are made with two hook stagings. The purpose is not to catch two fish at the same time, but simply a means of convenience to the fisherman in that it cuts down on the number of times he has to reel in to rebait the hooks.

In bay fishing the hooks can be tied directly to the leader stagings. The same method can be used around jetties unless there are strong currents running. Then attach the hooks to the stagings with snap swivels. This will allow the baits to spin in the current.

When it comes to surf fishing, snap swivels are a must at the hook stagings because the breakers and currents can make the baits spin furiously. On top of that be sure to use a good, smooth-working barrel swivel between the leader and line. These are a godsend when sinkers hold poorly and the terminal rig is rolled to the beach by breakers or currents. Without this barrel swivel the fisherman can end up with all sorts of line trouble. If he is using linen line, the terminal tackle roll to the beach may unravel the line. If braided synthetic line is used, the same roll will make the line prone to accidental knots, which always seem to come when making a cast. The same roll will kink monofilament line and cause it to tangle on the reel spool or around the rod tip or guides when slack is allowed.

7

Selecting Sinkers

One of the most important items in terminal tackle for channel bass fishing is the sinker. It must be heavy enough to provide weight for long casts, be shaped correctly to hold in the surf or strong currents, and still be inconspicuous enough so as to not make the naturally wary channel bass suspicious. Since these fish can be caught from the surf, in deep water around jetties and piers, and in shallow bays, the fisherman who desires to partake in all aspects of the sport must have three types of sinkers in a wide range of weights.

The surf fisherman must use sinkers reasonably streamlined to cut down wind resistance in making long casts. The sinker must have a shape that will permit it to dig quickly into the sand. The surfer must avoid using sinkers that are round, for these have a tendency to roll in the surf and currents.

The jetty and pier angler usually fishes in waters where there is no breaking surf. He has only the current to contend with and it is less of a problem than the one the surfer, who has a combination of breaking waves and currents fighting him, faces. If the pier fisherman is working an area that has a sandy bottom, he can use the same type sinkers used for surf work. Since piers extend out to reasonably deep water, and the fisherman does not have to reach for distance in casting, he can use lighter weight sinkers. If he is fishing around jetties, either from the topping proper or from a boat alongside, he is faced with having to use yet another kind of sinker. Weight is far less important here than in surfing and extremely long casts are not necessary.

Only a small portion of a jetty shows above the surface. The topping that shows may be ten feet across, but the base will slope out many feet to each side. A cross section of any jetty will show it as a pyramid with the top point cut off. In shallow water its top may be ten feet across with its base being 20 feet wide. The base becomes wider as the jetty is extended out into deeper water. Consequently, in a spot where the water may be 30 or 40 feet deep, the jetty cross-section may show a top of ten feet with a base of 60 to 100 or more feet. Width of the base depends upon the intensity of prevailing currents. The stronger the currents, the wider the base. A jetty with a narrow base in strong current water is very likely to be undermined and toppled. Jetty engineers don't like to have their reputations scuttled by undermining currents.

This wide base can present problems to the jetty fisherman. The typical surf sinkers with their flat surfaces, square corners, and copper wire tines can make for all sorts of headaches. They are prone to hanging up in the cracks and crevices in the rocks, and this can mean a lot of broken lines and lost terminal tackle. Therefore the jetty fisherman must use rounded or bomb-shaped sinkers free of flat surfaces, sharp angles, and broad bases.

The shallow bay fisherman who goes for channel bass with either surf or jetty sinkers is letting himself in for a lot of trouble. Surf and jetty water noises cover the sharp splash of big sinkers striking the water. Bay waters are far calmer and more silent, and the splash of a big sinker near a school of feeding rat reds can be enough to send the fish hightailing it out of the area. The bay fisherman must use much lighter sinkers. Since breaking waves are absent in bays and currents far less severe than in the surf, the sinkers need not be shaped to dig into the sand. You only need enough weight to make casting easy. Usually a quarter- to half-ounce sinker will suffice in bay fishing, whereas the weight around jetties and from piers would run one to three ounces, and the weights for surf fishing would run three to eight ounces or more.

For surf, pier, and jetty fishing the sinker can be attached in one of two ways. It can be attached to the very end of the leader with hook stagings tied a foot to 18 inches above it. This will keep the terminal tackle in one place on the bottom. Or the sinker can be rigged on the line just above the leader and hook stagings in such a manner that the line will run freely through the eye of the sinker. This is called a "fish-finder" rig. In using this setup, the sinker will hold in one place on the bottom, but the line running freely through its eye will allow the current to sweep the baited hooks around over a considerable area.

Although the bottom rigged sinker—small ones—can be used for bay action, it is not the best. By far the ideal bay rig is to attach the sinker firmly to the line immediately above the leader. Ideal sinkers for this kind of rig are the ringed, clinch-on, and lead coil, which simply rest on the bottom. The baited hooks are free to swing about in the light current, and this action aids in catching the attention of the fish. These sinkers are light enough so that when a fish picks up the bait and starts to mouth it, the pull won't be such to alarm the fish to the point of spitting the bait out.

SINKERS FOR THE SURF

SQUARE PYRAMID. On hard sand bottom this sinker lies on its side and line strain against sinker eye will cause the right angles of the sinker to dig into the sand like a plow. Square corners and flat sides of this sinker keep it from rolling in surf and current. It is excellent for fish-finder rig.

TRIANGULAR PYRAMID. This sinker has all the advantages of the square pyramid plus extra resistance to rolling in strong lateral currents. It is excellent for fish-finder rig. It is somewhat less easy than the square pyramid to cast into the face of a strong wind.

UPDEGROVE. This sinker bears the name of the man who designed it. It will bed easily in mud bottoms. On hard sand it lies on its side, and strain against its eye will cause it to dig quite deep into the bottom. This sinker is excellent choice for waters where surf is high and currents are strong. It also makes a good choice for the fish-finder rig. When reeling in it takes a good strain and jerk to free this sinker after it has dug into a hard sand bottom.

SURF SINKER. This sinker has unusual holding power and is

the author's choice for fishing in heavy surf and strong currents. The author has found that a four-ounce sinker of this type has the holding ability of an eight-ounce square pyramid. Its shape permits long casts. This sinker lies on its side. The copper wire tines quickly dig deep into even hard-packed sand and will cause the sinker to bury almost completely. The large eye located well above the sinker proper is ideal for using the fish-finder rig. If this sinker has a drawback, it is one of freeing it from the sand when one wants to reel in. It takes a long, steady, hard pull to break it loose from the bottom.

DIAMOND. This sinker is a fine choice for surf fishing when the breakers and currents are mild. It is a rather difficult sinker to cast into the face of a strong wind since its broad, flat face will often catch in gusts and dive quickly, shortening casts, or veer off to one side or the other of the spot when the fisherman seeks to drop his baited hook. This sinker has good resistance to rolling in strong lateral currents, but it is a poor choice for the fish-finder rig.

MULTIPLE TRIANGULAR. An excellent sinker for heavy surf and strong currents, which digs into the sand and holds well. But because it is a speciality sinker, it is not readily available in most tackle shops. Its compact shape makes long casts possible, but it is a poor choice for the fish-finder rig.

MULTIPLE-EYED CONE. Another speciality sinker that is hard to find. It holds well, but in relation to more conventionally shaped sinkers, it is quite expensive. Its cumbersome shape makes long casts a little difficult.

SINKERS FOR JETTIES AND PIERS

The square pyramid, triangular pyramid, and diamond are good choices for jetty and pier fishing if the bottom area is free of rocks. If rocks are abundant and lumped in piles, the following styles of sinkers are recommended.

DIPSEY. This is good to use for long casts over a rocky bottom. This sinker, however, has a tendency to roll in strong currents. It is suitable for the fish-finder rig in waters where currents are very light or absent.

BANK. Good choice for long casts and a sinker not prone to hanging up in rocks. It is a poor choice for the fish-finder rig. It also has tendency to roll on the bottom when currents are strong.

TOURNAMENT CASTING. Great for long casts because of its streamlined shape, but it is a poor choice when currents are strong because of its tendency to roll.

TURTLE. This sinker will hold well in relatively strong currents and is a good choice for the fish-finder rig.

EGG. This sinker must be rigged between the line and leader so the line can slip back and forth through its hole. It is an excellent choice for the fish-finder rig in rocky areas, but it is totally unsuited for use on hard sand bottoms if the current is strong. It is a poor choice for distance casting since the hook stagings that are rigged below it are likely to flip back and tangle the leader with the line above the sinker. In small sizes this sinker is a fine choice for fishing in the bays.

SINKERS FOR THE BAYS

Quarter- to half-ounce square pyramid, triangular pyramid, bank, dipsey, and tournament casting sinkers are acceptable if the fisherman desires to use a rigging on which the sinker is attached below the hook stagings. In order to permit the baited hooks to swing more freely in tidal action, a rig with the sinker above the leader is recommended. The following sinkers are recommended for such a rig.

RINGED. Rings or eyes on each end of this sinker permit it to be tied between line and leader. It lies flat on the bottom and will hold adequately unless strong currents are running. This sinker is an excellent one to use when fishing with live bait.

CLINCH-ON. This sinker is also called a dog-ear. It can be attached either to line or leader above the hook stagings. Ears are bent over to hold the sinker in place. It has less tendency to roll in currents than the ringed sinker, but care must be taken in bending over the ears so that sharp edges of the lead don't bite into the line or leader. This bite can weaken a line or leader enough to cause one to lose a big fish. This sinker is a good one to use in fishing live bait.

COIL. This is nothing more than a long strip of lead. It is coiled tightly around leader or line, and how much is used depends upon the weight the fisherman desires. It has a tendency to roll in strong currents and repeated casting will cause it to work loose. Fishermen using this type of sinker should check frequently in order to keep it from slipping up or down line.

Sinkers remind me of the depression days. I was too young at the time to be taken on surf channel bass trips by my father and his buddies. Yet I recall how they valued old spark plugs. They tied them together in gangs of two and three and used them for surf sinkers. And they worked, too.

A final word on modern sinkers. They come out of factory molds with rough edges and they are sold that way. It pays for the fisherman to knock off the rough edges—burrs—and smooth out the holes through which line is run. In spite of the fact that lead is soft, these edges can be sharp enough to chafe a line. This can be disastrous if the sinker is rigged between line and leader, for a chafed line can result in the loss of a good fish. Not a very pleasant thought to consider after one spends hours waiting for a good strike.

8

Natural Baits

Channel bass feed on both flesh and marine plant life. They will strike on a great variety of natural baits, but rather than go through a long list of them, some of which are difficult and costly to obtain, this chapter will be devoted to those most popular and easily obtainable. These include blood worms, crabs, shrimp, mullet, menhaden or mossbunker, squid, and clam. Practically all bait stands will have shrimp, mullet, and squid. Some are likely to have the other baits mentioned.

The fisherman interested in a complete work on natural salt-water baits, many of which are adaptable for channel bass fishing, can find complete descriptions and information on approximately 100 kinds in *Natural Salt Water Fishing Baits* by Vlad Evanoff, published by A. S. Barnes and Co. in New York in 1953.

The blood worm, which is most readily obtainable on the Atlantic coast, is a good channel bass bait for fishing around jetties, off piers, and in deep water. It is a poor choice for surf fishing for it can be snapped off the hook very easily. When blood worms are used, several should be rigged on the hook so as to make a glob of bait.

Two crab species—the blue and the calico—make good baits. When either is used, the pincher claws should be removed and the hook should be imbedded in the socket hole from which one of the claws is pulled. The blue crab can be used either hardshell or in its soft-shell or shedder stage. If the hardshell blue is used, it should be small in size—three to four inches —and it can be fished live. It is a good bait for jetty, pier, and

51

deep-water fishing. If small hardshell blues are unavailable, the large ones can be used, but the hard-back shell must be removed. This, of course, kills the crab and means that it is fished as dead bait. The hardshell, live or dead, is one bait that the bait-stealing fish won't bother. When you get a strike using a hardshell for bait, you know it is something big.

The blue crab makes an ideal bait when it can be obtained in its shedder stage, but be prepared to fork over money for it is expensive.

In the process of growing all blue crabs shed their hard shells several times a year. A crab is described as a shedder when it is ready to cast off its hard shell. The shell at this stage will break easily and expose the meat inside. When the crab completely sheds its shell, it becomes a soft-shell crab, and it is at this stage that it is most attractive to channel bass. It is also attractive to man, and as far as I am concerned, I would rather use the soft-shell crab for food than fish bait. Dipped in a batter and fried golden brown, it can be eaten whole—shell and all. An order of soft-shell crab—one and sometimes two to a plate—in a restaurant will cost from four dollars up, depending upon the class of the eating establishment. If the soft-shell is to be used for bait, it is best around jetties, piers, and in deep water. It must be cast out rather delicately to keep it from tearing off the hook.

The calico crab is much smaller than the blue and not so plentiful. It can sometimes be found at low tide. When the crab sees something approaching, it burrows into the sand. If you mark where the crab buried itself, it can be dug out with a rake or hand shovel. You can waste a lot of time hunting them, so the best practice to follow is to buy them from a bait stand.

Clams are readily available and make suitable bait, even in the surf. After the meat is removed from the shell, the hook should be looped several times through the hard part of the meat. This will keep the bait secure on the hook.

Squid are available at most bait stands. If they are small they can be used whole on the hook. Large squid can be made into several baits by cutting them into strips about three or four inches long and an inch wide. Don't throw away the head, for it makes a most attractive bait for channel bass. Squid are tough and hard to tear off the hook, and therefore a good bait for surf casting where a fellow has to put power and snap into a cast in order to get distance. Also, small bait-stealing fish have trouble tearing the squid off the hook, and you don't have to reel in repeatedly to re-bait.

The mullet is the most popular channel bass bait. It is easy to obtain and it can be fished either live or dead. Mullet are tough, and live mullet four to five inches long hold an unusual attraction for channel bass. In fishing the mullet live, the hook can be driven through the back before or behind the dorsal fin. Care must be taken so that the hook doesn't strike or break the backbone. If this happens, the mullet will die fast. A carefully hooked mullet will live for a long time. Another method of live-hooking mullet is to run the hook through both the upper and lower lips. This is a good rig for trolling. A third method, which I prefer, is to imbed the hook in the body near the tail. Again care must be taken to avoid hitting the backbone. I like this method because the mullet will do a lot of struggling to try to get off the hook, and this frantic action is helpful in attracting fish.

Small dead mullet can be fished whole. Run the hook through the mouth and out the gills and then imbed the point in the side or belly. These can also be hooked by driving the hook through the flesh in front of the dorsal fin or through the body near the tail.

When small mullet are unavailable and the fisherman is faced with using mullet 10 inches to a foot or more long, the bait must be cut into pieces. Some fishermen simply slice across the body and make a number of chunk baits about an inch and a half thick. It is best to remove the backbone from these chunks. Other anglers cut the mullet lengthwise and fillet off strips four to five inches long and about an inch wide. The hook is imbedded in one end of the strip, while the other end is left free to wave enticingly in the current. And as with the squid, don't throw the head away, for it makes a fine bait. On a number of occasions fishing parties that I have been in caught all their channel bass on mullet heads, while small live mullet fished alongside produced nothing. For all we know fish may be as discriminating about their food as man is. I love big, thick steaks, but every now and then I tire of them and go for a change of chicken, fish, and sometimes hamburgers.

Mullet can be kept alive for a long time if they are put into a live bait box and kept in the water. The bait will stay healthy and frisky as long as water circulates through the box.

When preparing mullet for chunk or strip bait, be sure to scale the fish. The scales are as tough as an old boot and they make cutting difficult and take the edge off a fishing knife. Mullet are excellent for surf fishing since they won't snap off the hooks on casts.

Menhaden, also called mossbunker, make excellent bait. Small menhaden can be hooked on whole in any of the same methods used with mullet. The fish can also be cut into two chunks by slicing in half diagonally. Use the head on the hook on one staging and the tail on the other. Menhaden are fatty and oily. If the bait is used whole, slice open the belly. The fat and oil that seeps out will create a nice chum slick. The drawback is that this same chum slick is a nuisance at times since it will attract a lot of fish species other than channel bass.

Shrimp make fine bait as long as the water is free of bait-stealers. If the pesky bait-stealers are around, a fellow will spend most of his time reeling in and re-baiting.

Shrimp range from little grass fellows an inch to an inch and a half long up to the jumbos measuring six to seven inches. The little grass shrimp is so small that it must be fished dead. The hook is threaded through the shrimp's body lengthwise in such a manner that the bait covers the hook's point, bend, and part of the shank. The larger shrimp are good for surf fishing and are threaded on the hook in the same manner as the small grass shrimp.

It is hard to use live shrimp in surf casting because such care must be taken in putting the bait on the hook. In surf casting the initial snap used in firing the bait seaward will pop a live shrimp off the hook. If the shrimp does remain on through the cast, it is certain to be pounded off by breaking waves.

Large live shrimp are superior when it comes to fishing around jetties, off piers, and in deep holes. Smaller live shrimp—two to three inches long—occupy the same exalted spot in bay fishing for rat reds.

There are several ways to hook live shrimp. One is to care-fully run the hook beneath the hard spike atop the shrimp's head. Be careful not to puncture the dark spot that appears in the head, otherwise the shrimp will die quickly. Another method is to run the hook through the first or second body joint section from the tail. My preference is hooking through the head spike for it enables the shrimp to swim about more naturally. This is particularly true if a float is used to keep the bait suspended a short distance off the bottom. Use of a float is recommended in fishing over flooded grass flats in order to keep the shrimp from swimming down and hiding around the stems of the grass.

Live shrimp for bait are more readily available along the Gulf Coast states than up the Atlantic seaboard. Shrimp are harder to keep alive than mullet or crabs. The shrimp must be kept in a live bait box in water and the water must flow freely through the box. Never crowd shrimp in the bait box, for over-crowding will result in the shrimp killing each other. The dead shrimp then contaminate the water and this will cause the remaining shrimp to die. If you have a live box advertised by its manufacturer as being large enough to keep 100 shrimp, play it safe by putting in only 50. If necessary purchase two live boxes. In the long run it will be a real economy, for live shrimp can be expensive.

I have seen live shrimp prices vary from two dollars a quart (about 60 to 70 shrimp three inches long) up to six dollars a quart. I have seen live jumbo shrimp sell for 10 to 12 cents each. You only waste money when you crowd shrimp in a live box and let them kill each other.

In the transportation of live shrimp, put either O-Tabs or a small chunk of ice in the container. The O-Tabs, which can be purchased for about 25 cents, put out a steady stream of oxygen when dropped in the water. The chunk of ice will lower water temperature in the container and make the shrimp less active and less likely to spear each other.

Compact and inexpensive pumps that operate off flashlight batteries are excellent for keeping bait alive and kicking. The units, most of which sell for less than five dollars, clip to the side or top of bait containers.

9
Artificial Lures

Channel bass can be caught on artificial lures, but it generally holds true that the bigger the fish, the less likely they will strike. Is it a case of the fish becoming educated with age and learning that artificial lures spell doom? Not true at all. The answer lies in the manner in which the fish feeds and the type of water it frequents.

Always remember that the channel bass is a bottom fish. It spends its time slowly nosing and rooting along the bottom. Although it can put on a burst of speed for a short distance, it is basically a slow swimmer. Although the fish has a strong tail, the shape is fan-like, which is a mark of slow swimming fish. The channel bass will chase after small baitfish that happen nearby, but it won't go hounding for great distances in pursuit of swiftly moving baitfish as will the king mackerel or bonita.

All of this means that one of the two basic requirements needed for a lure to be attractive to channel bass is that it has proper wiggle or action at a slow retriever. If a lure has to be retrieved swiftly in order to achieve proper action, it won't be very successful.

As is true with most bottom-feeders, the channel bass feeds in off-color or sandy water since such water permits small marine life to move about. When the water is gin clear, most of this same marine life goes into hiding. In a breaking surf, underwater visibility is reduced even more. Consequently the channel bass does most of its feeding by smell rather than sight.

Artificial lures have no smell, unless the fisherman decides to dip them in fish oils or dab them with some of the commercially prepared liquids that are supposed to attract fish. The only trouble here is that lures don't soak up the solutions. The lure might smell right for the fish, but I doubt if any of the odor remains on the lure after the first few feet or so of the retrieve. So for all practical purposes, smell on a lure is erased in a hurry. You can soak cut bait in these odor solutions and the smell will stay on these baits for a long time.

This brings us to basic requirement number two for the channel bass lure. Since it is being used in off-color or sandy water, visibility is restricted. A lure with a drab finish won't be seen by the fish unless it passes within inches of the fish. If lures are to be seen, the hardware must be flashy. In the case of spoons, the lure is all flash. If plugs are used, they should be silvery, red and white, or yellow in color. These are the colors that can be seen easiest in sandy water. And remember they must be retrieved slowly because of reduced visibility.

Furthermore the lure must have a pronounced enough wiggle so that some sort of underwater vibrations or sound waves are caused. These can be picked up through the fish's lateral line, and the fish is able to use this as a means of locating the lure—a sort of built-in sonar system. The system isn't restricted to the channel bass. All fish have lateral lines. An underwater plug with a propeller fore or aft is a good choice since the whirling blades will flash enough to provide visual attraction and will make a sound somewhat similar to the fin-fanning of a school of swimming baitfish.

Lure presentation is quite important. If the fisherman knows channel bass are moving along a certain trough in the surf, he should make his cast well beyond the trough and then work the lure back at an angle across it. Casting the lure right into the trough is likely to spook the fish if the lure happens to strike too close.

The same sort of presentation is made back in the bays where feeding fish often make their presence known by sticking their tails above the surface as they go rooting along the bottom.

The fisherman going for channel bass with lures will need a wide variety of plugs, spoons, jigs, and jig-worms. The plugs, spoons, and jigs should be light-colored and flashy, with white, yellow, and red being the best colors.

For surf, jetty, pier, and boat fishing in deep water, the fisher-man will need plugs and spoons ranging from three to six inches in length and weighing from two to four ounces. The weight is of particular importance in the surf where long casts are necessary. The plug is a poor choice for the surf when the breakers are big or one has to cast into a stiff wind. The wind will make long casts impossible, and the breaking surf will cause the plug to tumble wildly. This can put a lot of slack in a line, and the fisherman can have a strike and never know it. The spoon is a better choice for the surf, although it also has a tendency to tumble in heavy breakers. By far the ideal choice for a heavy surf is the jig. It is compact in size and has the weight necessary to enable long casts. It sinks quickly to the bottom where it will be relatively undisturbed by breaker action.

Another effective surf lure is the jig-worm. This is a leadhead with part of its body and the shank of the hook imbedded in a plastic worm. It has the necessary weight for long casts, it sinks fast, and it can be worked slowly along the bottom with a minimum of rolling interference from the breakers.

Although it still has to gain popularity, the plastic worm—the same worm that is such a deadly bait for black bass in fresh water—will reward the surf caster. It is most effective when used on a fish-finder rig. The sinker holds the rig out to sea, but the fish-finder permits the plastic worm to be carried around by the current. I have found the most effective colors in plastic worms to be black, purple, and red. You can turn the plastic worm into a sure-fire killer by running bits of yarn through its body. The yarn should extend out about a half-inch on each side. Use four or five of these on a six-inch long worm, and then soak the entire thing overnight in a jar of fish oil. The yarn will soak up and retain oil for a long time, and when cast out to sea the oil will seep out slowly and make a long slick that will attract fish to the lure. The only drawback with this type of lure is that it is attractive to a great many fish other than the channel bass. It is most effective when used in the fall of the year when the surf is relatively free of bait-stealers.

The same lures that produce in the surf can be used around jetties and off boats and piers. However, since extremely long casts are usually unnecessary, the fisherman can use smaller and lighter weight versions.

Size is of utmost importance when fishing for the small channel bass back in the bays. These fish won't take big lures. Plugs and spoons should not be over two inches in length with the weights in the quarter- and half-ounce range. Even smaller jigs can be used.

The plastic worm rigged naked except for hooks is a real killer on rat reds when they are feeding along the edge of flooded grass flats. The fisherman should make his cast so the worm will rest on the bottom just a few feet from the edge of the grass stand. Personally I don't recommend using the worm-yarn rig dipped in fish oil for bay fishing. Bays contain far more bait-stealers than the surf, and this rig will only keep you busy catching and unhooking unwanted fish.

I have caught a lot of rat reds on the plastic worm in bay fishing. The style of fishing is exactly like that for fresh-water black bass. Let the fish pick up the worm and start moving off with it before attempting to set the hook. My most memorable experience was that of catching rat reds on 16 successive casts one morning. The water was extremely high and only the tips of the grass above the surface showed the location of a salt grass flat that on normal tide conditions would have been totally exposed. The movement of the grass tips clued me on the location of the school of fish. I made casts ahead of and slightly beyond their direction of travel, and then I inched the worm back to a spot where the fish would cross.

I have caught channel bass on strictly surface lures. They were all rat reds back in the bays and never any of the bulls in the surf or around the jetties. Personally the surface plug or strict floater is a waste of time in redfishing. Because these fish are bottom-feeders, the surface lure is far away from where the fish normally feed. A surface lure that dives on retrieve is a good choice for it can be worked right down to the bottom.

Plugs, spoons, and jigs can be used in trolling for channel bass in deep water, with the spoon being the best choice. It should have a lot of flash and a slow wobble. To get down deep enough a trolling sinker should be rigged about three feet in front of the spoon. Because of the jolt involved when the strike comes in trolling, the fisherman should use a wire leader. And be sure to keep that drag setting light to prevent a broken line, leader, or rod tip. There is a heck of a jolt when a channel bass hits a trolled lure.

10
Fishing the Surf

Successful channel bass surf fishing is far more than just baiting hooks and casting out. If the surfer is to catch the big fish consistently, he must know their habits, the time of the year when they are most likely to move into the surf, and how to interpret surf conditions as to where to fish. Then to top it all off he must have infinite patience.

The man who goes to the surf for channel bass simply on impulse or plans to just while away an hour or so in hopes of getting fish will end up with very few. Channel bass fishing is inexpensive in terms of money spent for tackle and bait, but it is quite expensive if one puts a value on the hours spent, for the time between strikes is often long.

I have had occasions, even during the height of redfish runs on the Texas coast, when I have spent five or six hours fishing and have not lost a single bait or have a single strike. There have been other occasions when I latched onto big fish within a matter of ten minutes or so. In all fairness to the man who considers taking up surfing for channel bass, I must point out that long waits are far more common than catches in the first few minutes. It has often been said that surfing for channel bass is for men, not boys. It seems that boys just don't have the patience to fight out those long waits.

When natural baits are used, it is common to see surf fishermen stake several rigs out on sand spikes and then, while awaiting action, lounge in a beach chair with a good book. In this connection I had an amusing incident with my son on a surf trip. We were fishing at night—always the best time for reds—

and the weather was quite cold. I backed my station wagon to about 30 feet from the water, cast out, and then stuck the rods into rod-holders on the car's bumper. After about two hours without a single strike or loss of bait, I told my son I was going to lie down in the back of the station wagon and take a short nap. I had set the reel drags very light and put the click buttons on. In this way if a fish picked up the bait and ran, we would hear the click rattle like a machine gun. This happens to be a common style of surf fishing along the Texas coast.

I fell off into a sound sleep, and my son, who was just ten at the time, got sleepy, too. In he crawled and promptly fell off into snooze-ville. This must have been around 3 o'clock in the morning. The next thing I knew was when he shook me and said: "Hey, Daddy, it's daylight." And so it was.

I got up with a start and immediately checked the rods. Both were still secure in the bumper rod-holders, but the lines were broken. What had happened while we so blissfully slept was big fish, probably redfish, had picked up the baits and hooked themselves. They just swam away pulling out line—and we didn't hear the clicks chatter—and when they reached the end, they tugged hard enough to break the lines. One line broke right at the reel spool; the other at the rod tip. Those must have been mighty big reds. And for certain we were mighty sound sleepers.

The point is you don't have to tend the rod constantly when using natural bait, but at the same time you can't completely ignore it. The bumper rod-holders, which locked on the rod handles, were all that saved my rods and reels that night. Had I been using ordinary sand spike rod-holders, the fish certainly would have yanked the rigs out to sea, and I would have been poorer by about $95.

Although channel bass may be present in waters in a given area the year around, they are found in the surf in goodly numbers only at specific times of the year. Whether it is the Gulf Coast or the Atlantic seaboard, the best time for getting them in the surf is in the period from September through November. In the warmer waters bordering the Gulf Coast states, the surf runs occasionally extend well into December.

According to some studies made by marine biologists, the runs made into the surf in the fall are for the purpose of spawning. After the spawn run is completed, the huge schools break into small pods and return to deep water.

Water conditions must be right for the fish to move into the surf. The channel bass is an extremely wary fish, and one of the easiest to spook. If they can see or hear you, they will move out of an area. Consequently the big ones will stay away from the shoreline if the water is exceedingly clear and calm. Smaller fish ranging up to five pounds in size, however, will sometimes move into clear water. These smaller fish, often called "puppy drum" on the Atlantic seaboard and "rat reds" on the Gulf Coast, are not nearly as wary as the big fellows.

When the right months—September through November—roll around, the time to start fishing the surf is when it is up with pronounced lines of breakers and the water is sandy. The noise of the pounding surf works to the advantage of the fisherman in that it covers most normal noises he may make. The sandy water will permit the fisherman to get within casting range of the fish without being seen.

The habit of these fish is to move in schools parallel to the beach, with the school movement generally in the direction of the current. These schools move along in the troughs between the sandbars that run parallel to the beach. How close the fish move to the beach will depend upon tidal conditions. The bars and troughs are relatively close together near the beach, but as the water becomes deeper out to sea, the separation is much wider. On high or flood tides there is often enough water in the first off-beach trough for the fish to work. I have caught reds—big 20 and 30 pounders—from the first trough where the water was perhaps only two to three feet deep. At times I have seen their tails stick out of the water when they rooted for food on the bottom. When the tide is low, these fish are likely to be just outside the last seaward breaker during the spring and fall surf runs. In cases like this the fisherman faces a situation of having to wade out waist-deep in order to be able to cast far enough out to reach the fish. The pier fisherman has a real advantage in this situation.

Whether you are fishing the first trough or the last seaward one, you must know when to make your cast. This holds for natural baits as well as artificial lures. The cast must be timed so that the bait or lure hits the water on the sandbar past the trough you plan to fish. The terminal tackle must drop into this area right after a breaker has combed over the bar. If the cast is ill-timed and the terminal rig hits in front of the breaking wave, the wave itself is going to mess up the fishing. With artificial lures this breaking wave will cause the lure to tumble shoreward and put slack in your line. Under this condition you can have a strike and never feel it, and the ability to feel strikes when artificial lures are used is an absolute must. Big channel bass rarely hook themselves on artificial lures. When they feel the hardness of the lure, they will spit it out. Consequently when a strike or pickup is felt on the lure, the fisherman must immediately strike back in order to bed the hooks.

With natural baits channel bass often hook themselves. But the natural bait rig cast into a breaking wave is likely to be rolled back up to the beach before the sinkers strike bottom and dig into the sand. The water over a bar after a wave has passed is relatively calm. The rig will sink to the bottom, and then all the fisherman need do is to reel in enough line to pull the terminal tackle into the trough proper. This might mean reeling in 10 or 15 feet of line. The reeling in also helps in getting the sinker tines, flukes, or edges to dig into the sand and hold in place. This is important, for if the sinker hasn't dug in, the succeeding wave is likely to roll the terminal tackle shoreward.

Keeping the bait in place is one of the toughest aspects of fishing the surf, whether it is for channel bass or any of the other bottom-feeding species. The fisherman has two forces working against him: the breaking waves, which can roll the terminal tackle right back to him, and the lateral currents, which can roll the rig diagonally back to the beach. Keeping the bait where you want it is a matter of timing in making the cast and using the right sinkers. The matter of sinkers is discussed in the chapter entitled Selecting Sinkers.

Even during the height of a channel bass run in the surf, the fishing is much more than just casting out and waiting. The fisherman must have a knowledge of the area he is fishing. He must know the location of sandbars and troughs that run parallel to the shore. Let me point out that all references to sandbars

This is a homemade surf sinker. Wire tines cause it to dig deep into the sand. Note use of snap and swivel on hook to prevent line twist.

A hook-sinker rig like this is sometimes necessary to get down deep when trolling for channel bass. Beaded chain will permit bait to spin and will serve the same purpose as a swivel.

This lady angler had reason to be all smiles. The 25-pound channel bass gave her a thrilling battle in a round of surf fishing. (Photo courtesy Galveston Convention and Tourist Bureau)

The author has two rigs out in trying for redfish on a Texas beach. This is a common style of surf fishing in the Lone Star State.

When several rigs are used for surf fishing, the unattended ones are set in sand spikes. Note bait bucket conveniently rigged on spike between the two rigs.

When fishing the surf, always watch for hovering seagulls. They frequently work behind schools of big redfish to pick up food bits stirred up by the fish.

These two photos show the simplicity of the sand spike. Reel drag must be set light so rod will not be snatched out of the spike when the fish strikes.

Night is an excellent time to fish the surf, even when there is an absence of breaking waves. Large channel bass move into shallow water at night, even when the moon is bright.

On light tackle small redfish can be real battlers in the back bays. This Louisiana angler hooked his red near a stand of salt grass. On extreme flood tides small redfish move well up into the grass to feed. (Photo courtesy Louisiana Tourist Development Commission)

Note on this bay fishing rig the sinker is attached above the hook so as to allow the baited hook to swing naturally in the current. Fish this size make choice eating. (Louisiana Tourist Development Commission)

Rat reds, small fish up to about 18 inches in length, are popular with fishermen in the Gulf Coast states. These anglers are working a shallow Texas bay.

A nice string of two- to two-and-a-half-pound rat reds caught in a session of bay fishing. (Photo courtesy Galveston Convention and Tourist Bureau)

Texas sportsmen R. E. (Bob) Smith and Gus Loomis with six fine channel bass caught fishing the jetties. Smith is one of the men who figured in the building of the Astrodome in Houston and bringing major league baseball to Texas.

When redfish runs are on in full swing around jetties, anglers line the topping like pickets in a fence. This is a typical scene during the fall of the year on the Galveston, Texas, South Jetty.

are to those covered with a foot or more of water, and not to those that stand exposed above the surface.

You can determine the location of the bars and troughs by understanding the characteristics of waves. As waves move from seaward toward shore, the individual particles of water revolve in a circle. As long as the water is deeper than the diameter of this circle, the wave will not curl over and break. The exception to this comes in storms and hurricanes where the force of the wind causes towering waves to tumble and break.

When the depth of the water becomes less than the wave's diameter, the wave will curl and break. As it breaks, the force of the tumbling water churns the bottom on the shoreward side of the bar, causing the formation of a trough. This trough will slope up shoreward to another sandbar where the wave action is repeated all over again. Consequently wherever a wave breaks, there is a sandbar beneath it. The calmer water between breaking waves is where the troughs are located. Generally the fisherman will find that the bigger the waves, the deeper the troughs are between the sandbars.

These sandbars rarely run unbroken for miles. Lateral currents and the backwash from waves receding off the beach will cause small cuts to be formed in the bars. It is through these cuts, which connect the troughs with the open sea, that channel bass travel as they move from trough to trough. The only time they swim right in breaking waves is when they are alarmed and beat a hasty retreat to the security of deep water. These cuts can be located by watching for areas where lines of waves separate and the waters appear darker in color.

Channel bass are basically bottom-feeders. Note the configuration of the fish's head. It has a rather blunt nose for groveling in the sand, and it has a bit of an underslung lower jaw. These fish feed on marine shell life, sand worms, shrimp, crabs, and small baitfish, all of which are found on the bottom.

When the waves break, the force of the water churns up the bottom, naturally making it sandy. But more important as far as the fish are concerned, this churning action also exposes bottom marine life and makes it easy pickings for the fish.

What you find on the shore can give you a tip as to what is on the bottom offshore. For example, if the fisherman comes across a stretch of beach with patches of fine shells, he can reasonably assume that beds of this same shell life are immediately offshore in the surf. If there is no current running, the shell beds are likely to be straight out from their location on the beach. When lateral currents are running, the fisherman can determine the probable angle of the bed from the beach by casting out a line with a round sinker attached and then noting where the current rolls the sinker ashore. By remembering where he made the cast, and the relation of the spot where the sinker was rolled ashore to the shell patches on the beach, he can get a pretty good idea where the shell beds are located in the surf.

He might even try wading around in the surf to locate the shell when it crunches under his footsteps. This is not a recommended method, however, for the wading may spook off fish that are already feeding in the shell patch.

If he thinks he can place a marker on the beach opposite a shell bed in the surf and come back a day later to fish that spot, he is only fooling himself. Wave patterns and current directions and intensities vary from day to day. The shell beds of which I write are composed of small fragile shells about the size of a dime. Beds can be exposed by breaking surf one day, and then the next day with a change in wave patterns and currents, they can be completely covered with a foot or more of sand.

When channel bass schools are working in the surf, the fisherman should pay close attention to marine birdlife. Keep an eye peeled for gulls and terns. These birds are scavengers that pick up the leavings stirred up by fish. Whenever you see a flock of these birds wheeling in tight circles low over the water, you can be pretty sure that gamefish are feeding beneath them. Note the direction in which the birds are working, and then go about 100 yards and make your cast to a spot where they are likely to cross. Do this if you are using natural or dead bait, and wait for the school of fish to work to you. In the case of artificial lures, it is all right to cast into the water a little ahead of the direction in which the birds are moving. Remember the birds are picking up food left *behind* the school of fish. An artificial lure cast into a school of big channel bass won't spook them, but the natural or dead bait rig with its heavy sinker will. Thus it is important to stay ahead of the school when using such a rig.

11
Fishing the Bays

The fisherman seeking channel bass in excess of 10 to 12 pounds will find the pickings mighty slim if he tries for them back in the bays. But if he enjoys the smaller ones, the puppy drum and rat reds that run up to about five or six pounds, he will find plenty of action. Up the Atlantic seaboard he will find this bay fishing best in the spring and summer months. Because of generally warmer water and weather conditions he can find them the year around in the bays of the Gulf Coast states, especially in Florida and Texas.

After these fish get to around 10 to 12 pounds in size, they vacate the bays to spend the remainder of their lives in relatively deep water just off the coast. Although some big channel bass are occasionally caught 30 to 40 miles out to sea, the fish is normally an inshore inhabitant of deep water near the coast.

In the chapter Fishing the Surf, I mentioned that small reds are not nearly so wary as their adult kin. This is true when it comes to the surf and quite likely because the general noise of the breaking surf covers other noises alien to fish. Back in the bays the rat reds are just as wary as the big fellows in the surf. My personal feelings are that the absence of surf noises in the bays allows the fish to hear, or more correctly feel through its lateral line and swim bladder, foreign noises. Consequently the fisherman going after these fish in the bays must do so with quiet and stealth.

Although there may be a lot of walking involved, the fellow who wades the shallow bay flats has a better chance of getting these fish than does the man in the outboard powered boat.

This is not a condemnation of outboards for fishing. Rather it is an indictment of the manner in which so many fishermen use the outboard. Far too many are prone to racing into an area at full speed and not cutting the throttle until they are a few yards from the place they plan to fish. No wonder the fish vacate the premises and head for more serene surroundings.

If the outboarder would just reduce throttle when he is still several hundred yards away from the spot and then approach it with the motor barely ticking over, he stands a good chance of not alarming the fish. If a fellow can paddle silently without bumping the side of the boat or unduly splashing the water, he would be even better off to paddle in that final hundred yards. The fisherman must always remember that water is five times denser than air and is a good conductor of sound. The sound made by bumping a paddle against the boat's side is rather sharp and sudden. It can be far more alarming to the fish than the slow ticking of an outboard motor. I feel outboards are used so much in the bays that the fish have become somewhat accustomed to them, unless the motors run wide open.

Likely places to fish in the bays are far easier to find than they are in surf fishing. Hydrographic and navigation charts, which list reefs, bars, cuts, channels, and approximate water depth in feet, are invaluable. They show quite accurately the points, coves, and contours of the shoreline. These charts can be purchased at marine supply houses, yacht basins, and some sporting goods stores.

Now for the places to fish. Regardless the tides, never pass up fishing the shell reefs, especially if they are live. On flood tides the fish are likely to work atop the reefs if they are covered by sufficient water. When the tides are low, the same fish are likely to be found in the deeper water that borders the fringes of the reefs.

Cuts and channels are must places to fish on low tides, for on falling tides rat reds will always move back toward deep water. In bays where the difference between high and low tides may amount to several feet, some flats fishable on normal tides may have only a few inches of water over them on the low tide. As tides fall, the fish move away from the shorelines.

It is the reverse on rising tides, especially on abnormal flood tides. Then the fish fan out over the well-flooded flats and move right up to the shoreline, working well up into bayous and coves. If the tide is an abnormal flood one, then the fish are very likely to move right into the salt grass. I have seen times when schools of rat reds moved into flooded salt grass flats and caused the tips of the grass showing above the surface to wave back and forth. These fish moved into the grass stands to feed on the small shell and marine life clinging to the base of the vegetation. If you doubt this, catch some rat reds out of grass stands and carefully examine the contents of their stomachs. Compare what you find with the marine life attached to the stems of grass.

Small channel bass travel in schools like the older adults, and they often make their presence known in bays the same as with the adults in the surf. The fisherman will find this to be the case when fishing the flats and salt grass stands on flood tides. Often the schools will move along in water just a foot or so deep. They will create surface V's when they swim fast, and when they root to feed on the bottom, their tails will often fan above the surface. The least bit of sudden or foreign noise in a situation like this will send the fish swiftly finning out to the security of deep water. In any case the fright will cause the school to cease feeding for quite some time, so even if the fisherman knows where they are headed, he stands little chance of getting any by chasing after them. Just forget that school and start looking for another. There are some species of fish that can be caught by chasing after them. The channel bass, however, is not one.

Care must be exercised in the manner in which the bait or lure is presented when fish are found working on the flats. Natural bait, whether live or dead, presentation differs from that used with lures.

Natural bait presentation will be discussed first since it ranks first with most channel bass fishermen. Use just enough sinker weight to permit easy casting. Keep in mind that the plunk of a big lead sinker in the water can make a sharp enough noise to spook rat reds. Rig the sinker two to three feet above the baited hook so that the bait can swing about freely in the current. When the bait is rigged so that it will move about, rat reds are more apt to hit it hard and hook themselves. With the bait that is rigged above the sinker and fished tight-line so that it is virtually motionless, the fish is more apt to mouth it gently. And if the fish feels something sticky or foreign in its mouth, it will spit the whole works out.

Note the direction in which the school of fish appears to be moving. Then make your cast about 25 or 30 feet ahead of the school. Let the fish work to the bait. Never attempt to cast the bait right into the school, for if you should happen to hit one of the fish, the whole school will skedaddle in a hurry.

Lures make a splash, too, when they strike the water, but the noise is not nearly so sharp or jolting as that of the lead sinker. Consequently artificial lures can be cast considerably closer to the working school of fish. Again note the direction in which the school is moving and make the cast slightly in front of but beyond the fish. Then retrieve the lure so that it crosses just a few feet in front of the fish or even through the front part of the school. Remember the lure is made to look like some sort of marine life. Since it is wiggling and wobbling in the water, rat reds will strike at it sharply rather than nose or mouth it as they do with natural dead bait fished on the bottom. The lures must be ones that attain their proper action on a slow retrieve. Channel bass, even little ones, rarely chase after swiftly retrieved lures.

And now again comes the point where the men are separated from the boys. A good bay fisherman can catch a number of rat reds out of a single school. The tyro, however, will get one— maybe two. The separation point between the accomplished fisherman and the tyro comes in the manner in which the fellow plays the fish after it is hooked.

The normal reaction when the bait or lure is hit is to strike sharply by bringing the rod to a perpendicular position to the water. This is the correct way to apply the force needed to drive the hook tines into the fish's flesh. Under normal circumstances with most species of fish the angler scraps the fish all the way in with the rod held nearly perpendicular to the water or at least at an angle so the rod tip and line form a 90-degree angle.

You can't do this with rat reds in shallow water and still expect the remainder of the school to remain around. The rod tip held high will pressure the fish up near the surface where it will create a commotion splashing around. This is enough to break up a school and cause the remaining fish to scatter.

The proper way to bring in a red hooked in shallow water is to dip the rod tip to the surface of the water. Some of the old pros go so far as to stick their rod tips below the surface. The 90-degree angle between rod tip and line can be maintained by the wade fisherman if he simply sticks his rod tip off to his right or left. The fellow fishing from the boat can do the same plus have the option of sticking the rod tip straight down in the water. The purpose is to keep the fish away from the surface as much as possible. True, a fish fighting at the surface presents a dramatic scene of big splashes and curtains of spray. But all this commotion is enough to send the rest of the school to parts unknown.

Most all bays have shorelines that are cut by small bayous and fingers that wind well back into the marshes. Usually these are comparatively deep in relation to the adjacent flats. One of the peculiarities of rat reds is for them to venture far back into the marshes if there is sufficient water in these bayous and fingers. This is certain to happen on extreme flood tides. The bayous and fingers are worth fishing, but it should be done by walking along the banks and not by wading in the water. I have caught a lot of rat reds from fingers three or four feet deep and only 20 or 30 feet wide.

When the tide starts to fall after flood water, an excellent place to fish is at the mouths of these same bayous and fingers. This is best done from a boat anchored right outside the mouths. When the tide starts to fall, and especially on a fast drop, the rat reds that ventured almost back to the cattle grazing in the prairie will come funneling out bent on getting to safe, deep water.

If a fisherman is at the mouth of a bayou at the right time, he can get into some mighty fast action. This kind of fishing is most likely to occur in the spring and fall when the difference between high and low tides is the greatest.

12
Fishing the Jetties

Good channel bass fishing can be found in the deep holes and channels around jetties, particularly those that extend seaward several miles. Along the Atlantic seaboard from Florida northward, this kind of fishing is fair to good for approximately nine months each year. It is poorest in the period from December through February. Around jetties in the Gulf Coast states this fishing can be year around.

These jetties are located on all coasts and may extend from 100 yards to four or five miles in length. For example, there are two types of jetties at Galveston, Texas, where I live. The two-mile South Jetty and five-mile North Jetty parallel to protect the Galveston Ship Channel entrance. In front of the Galveston Seawall proper there are a number of rock jetties that extend out about 500 feet. These jetties, which are known locally as rock groins, are for the purpose of protecting the Seawall foundation from being undermined and eroded by tides and currents.

These short groins offer excellent action in the fall when the channel bass invade the surf. The North and South Jetties, which extend out to water 35 to 40 feet deep, offer good year round fishing for channel bass. Similar harbor entrance protection jetties are found all along the Gulf and Atlantic coasts. When water and weather conditions permit, these jetties can be fished from the toppings or from boats nearby.

Jetty topping fishing, especially on the long ship channel ones, should not be attempted unless the fisherman is as nimble and surefooted as a mountain goat. Even when dry these huge rocks can be dangerous when one has to hop over cracks and crevices

72

and step up or down to rocks lying at various angles. When water washes over these rocks, the walking becomes even more dangerous. There are times when water washes so consistently over the rocks that they will be covered with growths of slippery moss. Shoes or waders with felt soles will aid one in keeping footing, but even then the wise fisherman picks his way slowly and carefully. Waters around jetties are deep and the currents are dangerous, and it is advisable to carry along some sort of life-saving gear. The inflatable vest types are all right as long as they are not rubbed sharply against the barnacle-covered rocks. Jackets filled with kapot are a better choice, although they can be cumbersome. A good many jetty fishermen now wear the water-ski belts, and although they are not Coast Guard approved for carrying in a boat, they will do the job for the fellow who slips off the rocks.

Live or dead bait and lures can be used for channel bass around jetties. Care must be used in keeping the terminal tackle free of underwater snags, and even if a fellow knows an area, he is bound to lose a few terminal rigs to the snags. It is just something that has to be accepted in jetty fishing.

Extra care is necessary in playing a big channel bass. The fisherman will have to walk up and down the rocks in moves to keep the fish from swimming under or alongside barnacled rocks that can chafe and cut lines like hot butter.

The man who does his fishing from the jetty topping should use a seven- to eight-foot-long rod that has considerable backbone. This is needed for lever action in horsing fish away from snags and out from under overhanging rocks. This is a chore that can be complicated when swells crash against the rocks and send showers of spray over the fisherman. The next item is a long-handled gaff. This by far beats a wide-mouthed landing net. The webbing of these nets always seems to tangle in rocks, chafe, and tear.

The poorest time to do jetty fishing is when the water is dead calm, the tide is at a standstill, and there are no currents. Under these conditions the fish are certain to scatter, and will work some distance out from the jetty proper. If the fisherman knows the location of holes alongside the jetties, he should seek his fish there.

When currents are running, the fish often move in very close to the rocks. I have caught channel bass by casting out as little as 20 feet from the rocks. These currents form rips and eddies around the underwater portion of the jetties, which often trap schools of baitfish and at the same time pull small marine life free from the rocks proper and swirl it around freely. All this marine fodder will bring the fish in close.

If conditions are such that swells break against one side of a jetty and send cascading water to the other side, there are two likely places for the fisherman to try. Fish close to the rocks on the breaking side, where baitfish will be forced in. On the opposite side the cascading and rushing water will carry baitfish away from the rocks. Consequently cast further out.

Boat fishing a jetty is far easier and safer than fishing from the topping. The boat gives the fisherman mobility to cover a wider area and it gives him the advantage of getting to many places completely out of reach of the rock jumper. The boat fisherman is certain to land more fish than the rock jumper, for in fighting a big fish, the boatman has the advantage of working the fish away from rocks that can chafe and cut lines.

The boat fisherman, however, must own up to the fact that he is going to have anchor troubles. If currents are strong, he will need to put out a lot of anchor line in order to make the hook hold. To play it safe he should carry sufficient anchor line to equal six times the maximum depth of the water fished. This is the safe ratio recommended in most boating manuals.

When the boatman anchors in near the rocks and his anchor drops down into the rocky part of the jetty that fans out, there is always the risk of the anchor fouling. Sometimes this means a lost anchor, unless a fellow is reckless enough to strip off his clothes and dive down to free the hook. This is not only reckless, it is also stupid in strong currents that are the rule around jetties.

The boatman who fishes consistently around jetties should use one of a number of brands of shear-pin anchors. These are anchors that can be freed by tugging hard enough to break the pins. When the pins break, the anchor flukes will reverse and usually it can be freed.

One way to beat the jetties is to use a rock anchor. This is simply a homemade anchor that frees quite easily from snags.

It is so inexpensive that if it is lost, the money involved is negligible. A simple rock anchor can be made with four lengths of iron building rods. Each rod should be three to four feet in length. The rods are then either welded or bonded together with stout wire at one end and again in the middle. The free ends are then bent outward to form a hook. The completed assembly looks like a grappling hook. The tines will hold securely in the rocks, but the anchor can be freed by strong tugs and jerks that will straighten out the tines. Then all one has to do to use the anchor again is to bend the tines outward.

13
Fishing from Piers

When it comes to pier fishing for channel bass, the number of folks using this method will almost equal the number who fish the surf from the beach. In a way pier fishing is a kind of surf fishing. Personally I don't care for it because I don't like to fish under crowded conditions, which are usually the rule on piers. However, I am not going to knock it for channel bass fishing, for it does hold some advantages for the fisherman if he has the temperament to put up with some of the things that invariably will happen in a crowd. Perhaps I should list these problems first and then go into details on the advantages of pier fishing.

The man who needs room for casting will run into trouble on a crowded pier. If he likes to fight big fish on light tackle, he is going to encounter the wrath of neighboring fishermen when his fish swims around and tangles lines. And then there is the case of the same fish with hooks from two different lines in its mouth. Man, I have seen some beautiful fist fights in trying to settle the issue as to which baited hook the fish hit first.

But despite the disadvantages of pier fishing, there are many advantages offered. First off the pier extends out into deep water and enables the fisherman a better shot at year around fishing for channel bass. He can fish halfway out on the pier when the fish are running in the surf, and when the fish go to deep water he can move out to the end. Even during the spring and fall surf runs, there will be times on low tides when the only folks who catch channel bass are those fishing the deep water from the pier T-heads.

Pier fishing is far less strenuous than true surf fishing. A fellow doesn't have to use heavy sinkers to hold the bait out to sea. He doesn't have to make long casts or time them so the bait doesn't plunk down in front of a breaking wave. Wading in the surf is completely eliminated, and he can reach the bar or trough he desires without getting wet. This is an advantage of the first magnitude when it comes to fishing in the fall of the year. True surf fishing can get mighty uncomfortable in cold weather. Pier fishing will also mean the fellow doesn't have to buy extra gear like sand spikes, bumper rod-holders, or waders.

Automobiles can be driven on a number of our coastal beaches, yet there are times in the year, usually in the spring and fall, when tides are so high that they prohibit beach driving. Consequently this knocks out the surf fisherman completely unless he has permission to cross private property immediately behind the beach. This is becoming more of a problem every year as more and more beach front property is gobbled up for private developments. This same flood tide that keeps the surfman off the beaches won't bother the fellow who fishes from the piers.

The pier fisherman must use a fairly stout rod for battling fish when they move close to the pier pilings. He will need the leverage to force the fish back into the clear. He should use a wire leader, for when the fish is in close to the pilings it is liable to scrape the leader against the barnacles. A monofilament leader would part in a hurry.

Public and free fishing piers offer the fisherman a minimum of fishing tools. These piers really amount to little more than a railed platform that extends out to deep water. Therefore a fellow must take along his own gear for landing big fish. This can be either a large ringed net that can be dropped into the water and then lifted up when the fish is led over it, or a long-handled gaff. The gaff is the easiest to use if the fisherman doesn't have a buddy around to lend a hand. The pier fisherman need not worry about this gear when fishing from private piers since this equipment is readily available on the fishing deck. Furthermore the better fee piers also have attendants on hand to assist in decking big fish. Their operators will do everything they can to aid the fisherman because they want his repeat business. These charge piers also have bait, terminal tackle, and snacks for sale, and many also rent rods and reels.

Fees vary from a low of 50 cents to three dollars a day. Many sell season passes, which range from 10 to 25 dollars a year, good for the entire family. The fisherman who desires elbow room would do well to select those piers charging the higher prices, although this doesn't always mean the fishing is that much better. I know of some public free piers that are located in far better places for good channel bass action than some of the charge piers in the same general area. Finding the best piers is a matter of checking with the native fishermen in a given area. Don't take one man's word for a pier; seek the opinion of a half dozen or so of the natives. This is the way to go about it on the public free piers. On the well-operated charge piers, complete records are kept on big fish catches, and the pier operators see to it that these records are well publicized.

14

The Strike and Fight

Small channel bass strike sharply. They are far less prone to nose and mouth baits as do the big fellows ranging in excess of 20 pounds. The big bulls will strike hard if they are traveling in schools and there is competition for the bait. However, if the fish is a loner, it will pick up the bait, mouth it, and then swim off slowly with it. If this fish feels an immediate strain on the bait, it is likely to drop it and move off. If the line strain is light, the fish is more likely to take the bait well into its mouth, and then comes the time to set the hook.

If the fish are not moving in schools, the best terminal rig to use is the fish-finder. When the fish picks up the bait, line will travel freely through the eye of the sinker. After the fish moves off a half dozen or so feet, the fisherman should then rear back on the rod to set the hook. One good strike with the rod is enough, although there is nothing wrong with several additional but lighter strikes. But the fisherman who rears back for all he's worth a half dozen times is likely to lose his fish. If the hook is bedded in the fish's lip or a tender part of its mouth, the additional heavy strikes may tear the hook out. Should the hook be bedded in solid, tough flesh, these extra strikes may wear a hole in the flesh and the hook may drop out if line slack is allowed during the fight.

Because of the long waits between strikes, most surfers seeking channel bass go out with anywhere from two to a half dozen rods and reels. They bait and fish them all. If a fellow is using three or more rigs, the common style is to cast one or more to the far seaward trough. Another will be dropped into the second trough from the shoreline. The really good fisherman also drops baited hooks into the first trough from the shoreline, even though it may only be 40 or 50 feet from the beach. Tyros would be amazed if they could be on hand to witness how many 20- and 30-pounders are caught so close to the beach.

Naturally the surfer with a half dozen rigs out can't be expected to hold them all at the same time. One he will hold, while the others are fitted into sand spikes that are firmly bedded in the sand right at the edge of the water. These spikes are four- to five-foot lengths of metal rod or angle iron with a foot-long length of pipe welded or bolted to one end. The inside diameter of the pipe is large enough so the butt of the rod can be inserted into it.

By wiggling back and forth while pushing down, the sand spike can be worked to a depth of about two feet in the sand. It should be set at enough of a slant so that when the rod is inserted it will lean seaward at an angle of about 70 to 80 degrees. An angle of less than 45 degrees can result in a lost rod and reel if a big fish hits sharply and takes off. In addition to seeing this happen to other fellows at least several dozen times, I had it happen to me once.

After the cast is made, the fisherman walks back to the sand spike with the reel in free spool. He then engages the gears and takes enough turns on the crank so there is no slack line that can be whipped back and forth in the surf. Next he inserts the rod firmly into the butt-holder on the sand spike.

Now comes the most important part of the operation. If using a conventional revolving spool reel with a strong click that will hold against existing surf conditions, back the drag all the way off. If the clicker won't keep line from paying out, then tighten down the drag just enough to hold. This is extremely important when the rod is to be left untended. With a surf spinning reel the drag setting should be just heavy enough to keep line from being pulled out by breaker or current action.

You can be a hundred feet down the beach when a fish strikes and the untended rod and reel will be safe. The arcing of the rod tip and the noise of the clicker will give you ample warning to get back to the rig in a hurry. The first thing to do even before taking the rod out of the sand spike is to tighten the drag so that you can make that initial strike without having line spool off the reel.

After the hook has been set readjust the drag again. Tighten it down enough so that line can be retained on the reel when the fish moves parallel to the beach, but light enough for the fish to take off line if it decides to run seaward. If the drag is tightened all the way down, the fisherman runs the risk of tearing the hook out of the fish's mouth or breaking the line.

Runs made by big channel bass only seem long. Actually they only run 50 or 60 yards in any one direction before sheering off toward another point of the compass. The initial run, perhaps even the second and third runs, will be made to seaward. After that the runs will be back and forth parallel to the beach with most of the runs being in the direction of the current.

Therefore, reels with 500 or 600 yards of line are not necessary. If the fisherman has 100 yards of line left on the spool after he makes his cast and walks back to the sand spike, he is in excellent shape. My favorite surf reels are the Penn 9, Penn 209, and Mitchell 402. The two Penn reels are conventional revolving spool reels, and the Mitchell is a spinning reel. The Penn 9 has 200 yards of line, the 209 has 250 yards, and the Mitchell is filled with 350 yards. The line test on each reel is 20 pounds. The only reason I have the Mitchell filled to capacity is because casting is easier with a full spool. I had the Penn 9 stripped bare of line one time. That was when I stuck the rod in a bumper rod-holder and went to sleep. (This incident is related in detail in Chapter 10, Fishing the Surf.)

The fight of a big channel bass isn't all one of a steady strain. If the fish finds it is unable to win freedom by swimming seaward, it will start making runs back and forth parallel to the beach. If there is a heavy surf running, the fish is likely to run in with a breaking wave and then swing back seaward. In this situation the fisherman must be able to reel in line fast enough to keep a strain on the fish and to prevent slack. If necessary, the fisherman can start walking backward up the beach. Yet at the same time the angler must maintain a drag setting light enough to yield line and cushion the shock when the fish turns and makes its seaward run.

No one can predict how long a big channel bass will fight.

I once landed a 41-pounder—on 20-pound test line—in five minutes. That fish hardly had any fight and must have been sick, lazy, or old. Another time I had to struggle for a half hour with a particularly stubborn and strong 20-pounder. Fifteen to 20 minutes is about average for landing a 30-pound fish on conventional tackle. If a fellow is a light spinning tackle buff with 10-pound test line, then he had better figure on spending the better part of an hour with a big fish.

I would estimate that about half of the channel bass lost are fish that gain their freedom when they are in water just a few feet deep. This is when the fisherman sees his fish and gets careless. It's at this stage that many fishermen make the terrible mistake of tightening down the drag. Just because the fish is slowly finning in shallow water, this doesn't mean it has lost all its fight and is ready to surrender. The fish is almost certain to bolt seaward when it sees and hears the approaching fisherman. If the drag setting is too tight, the hook will tear out of the fish's mouth or the line will break.

Pay attention to drag settings while the fish is still battling well out to sea. When a fish starts a run and the fisherman looks down and sees line streaking off the reel, there is a tendency to panic and make the disastrous mistake of tightening down the drag to slow the run.

This is the wrong thing to do. If the run is a particularly long one—and 70 yards would be for a big channel bass—the proper thing to do is to gradually loosen the drag as line peels out. Don't think for one moment that this is lessening tension on the fish. It is not. Instead it is keeping the strain constant. This is easy to understand when you consider the mechanics of forces on a spindle. As the diameter of the spindle decreases, the amount of force necessary to revolve the spindle against the friction applied increases. The reel spool has a fixed diameter metal or plastic spindle. But when line is spooled on the reel, the line that is wound around the spindle becomes part of the spindle and increases the diameter. This means that the more line wound on the reel, the less force needed to peel line off against a given drag setting. When the channel bass makes its run, the fish is taking line off the spool, thereby decreasing the diameter of the overall spindle (reel spindle plus line). Therefore the more line the fish takes off, the more the drag increases. It can reach the point of being too much drag, and the hook is torn free from the fish's mouth or the line breaks. So when the fish makes a long run, gradually loosen the drag. The purpose of the drag is not to completely halt a fish's run. Its purpose is to slow the fish down and wear it out by steady pressure.

Even when the fish is in sight and just a few feet from the beach, play it as though it had all the fight and vigor it possessed when first hooked. Keep a steady strain on the line and let the fish tire itself out. You will know when this happens. The fish will roll over on its side or back when waves roll over it. If the waves are substantial, work the fish around until its head is pointed toward the beach and then walk backwards as a wave rolls over it. The line strain and force of the wave will often bring the fish right up on the sand.

If the fish is a big one, wade out and bring it in with a gaff hook. Don't try grabbing the fish with your bare hands. The scales are too tough and slippery for one to get a firm grip at the base of the fish's tail. The fish is too big to lip like a black bass. If you have a big hand and strong grip, you can grab the fish by the top of the head by inserting your thumb in one eye socket and your index finger in the other. It's okay to do this if you plan to keep the fish for food or mounting, but if it is to be released to live and fight again another day, skip this grip for it can badly damage the fish's eyes. By all means keep your hands out of its gills. They are sharp and can inflict painful cuts and scratches.

If you like to catch fish that jump and tail-walk on the surface, the channel bass isn't your meat. This fish is a sub-surface fighter all the way. In all my years of catching these fish—and at this writing they total 30—I have seen only two hooked channel bass jump completely out of the water. The first time I saw this was in fishing around a jetty. A fellow in a nearby boat tied into a large bull and during the course of the fight the fish jumped completely out of the water. This was indeed rare for the depth of the water was around 30 feet.

The second jumping redfish was one that I caught from the surf on Galveston west beach. The fish was hooked in about four feet of water. I had fought it perhaps 10 or 15 minutes when

I saw two dark fins cutting the surface and heading toward my fish. All of a sudden there was a shower of spray and right behind it was my redfish going high into the air. One dark fin and part of the back of a huge shark then showed above the water. My fish hit the water with a splash and with all of its fight gone I was able to reel it quickly to the beach. My fish, minus a foot of its tail, weighed 27 pounds. I don't think the fish really jumped but just got pushed by the shark. I am still amazed that the sharks didn't move right back in when it hit the water and tear it to pieces before I could get the fish to the beach. Perhaps the two sharks were arguing between themselves about the tail portion that had been bitten off.

When it comes to the rat reds, the fisherman won't get much of a fight if he uses heavy tackle. If the fish is well hooked, the angler can simply horse it in. But if the same fish is caught on correspondingly light tackle, it will give a good account of itself. Its runs will be around ten to fifteen yards before making direction changes. If the water is shallow, there may be a lot of surface splashing that could give the tyro the impression that the fish is a surface scrapper.

These small fish can be brought in with a landing net, small gaff hook, or fish-grippers. Two and three pounders can be landed easily by simply tiring them out and then grabbing them by the lower lip à la black bass fashion.

The bay fisherman who uses a whippy rod with a light bait-casting, spinning, or spin-cast reel can have a barrel of fun battling rat reds.

15

How to Surf Cast

The fellow who fishes for channel bass in the bays and off jetties, piers, and boats can learn to cast properly in rather short order. He uses relatively few muscles in his body in this kind of casting. In bay fishing the arm plays the key role. When fishing from jetties, piers, and boats, the fisherman uses both arms and the upper part of his body since he will be fishing with tackle considerably heavier than that used in the bays. He is not trying for extreme distance in any of these kinds of casting, and his casts will fall into a 25- to 30-yard range.

When it comes to surf casting, 25 to 30 yards is short. The average is closer to 50 yards, with those in the seventy- to eighty-yard range considered fairly long. The "hot stuff" surf fisherman is the one who can reach out consistently to 100 yards.

This quest for distance makes surf casting something special and quite an art. It isn't easy and it takes time to learn and master. It is a cast in which timing, coordination, and the entire body come into play.

The most important part in the cast is the position of the feet. They must be placed properly so that the position of the body is such where the natural actions of muscles are used most efficiently. The left foot should be parallel to the edge of the water with the left shoulder pointed at the spot where the fisherman intends to drop his bait.

A follow-through as in golf is necessary. When the fisherman is prepared to make his cast, his weight is initially on his right foot with a slight bend at the right knee. Immediately after the cast is started and the rod is brought forward, the fisherman's body begins to swivel at the waist and his weight is transferred to the left foot. The power or pressure exerted on the cast then extends from the left foot upward through his body. Then his right foot comes forward in a normal follow-through motion to a point directly in front of the left foot. The right foot also takes the weight of the fisherman's body as the cast ends. If you go through the procedure slowly, you will see that the entire body is utilized in this kind of casting.

The casting procedure just described is for the right-handed fisherman. The left-handed fisherman need only flip-flop foot placement with the right foot being placed parallel to the edge of the water and the right shoulder pointed at the spot of aim at the start of the cast.

At the start the rod is pointed directly behind the fisherman with the bait or lure suspended three to four feet from the rod tip top. The rod is held in a position so that the right and left hands are about level with the shoulders. Then the bait or lure is dropped on the beach sand as the fisherman puts his weight on his right foot and slightly bends his right knee.

Actually the cast starts slowly and picks up momentum until the rod is pointed almost straight up. The right-handed fisherman then at this point pulls down hard with his left hand and pushes forward with the right. Remember this is reversed if the fisherman is left-handed. This quick pivot action puts a deep bend in the rod tip, which when it snaps back to its normal straight position gives the terminal tackle extra forward thrust. This extra thrust from the tip is what gets the distance on the cast. A split second after the rod tip snaps forward, the fisherman eases off thumb pressure on the reel spool so that line is free to follow the pull of the sinker. Never take the thumb completely off the spool, otherwise a backlash is certain. Light thumb pressure throughout the cast must be maintained to keep the reel spool from over-spinning. Just before the sinker hits the water increase thumb pressure to the point of completely stopping the spool. This pressure increase is gradual, otherwise a sudden stop would result and snap the sinker back beachward. At the end of the cast the rod is pointing right at the spot where the sinker hits the water. Surf casting really isn't difficult. It just takes practice and coordination.

The amount of pressure one puts into the cast depends on four things: distance desired, weight of sinker and terminal tackle, kind of bait used, and type of surf rig used. The greater the distance and sinker weight involved, the greater the need for pressure. More pressure is needed with the conventional revolving spool reel than with the open-face spinning reel. The surf spinning reel will allow for casts as long as the conventional reel but with less sinker weight.

Great pressure can be applied in the cast if the bait is dead or hard or if artificial lures are used. Soft baits are likely to be snapped off the hook when great casting pressure is applied quickly. This same kind of pressure may kill live bait.

Surf casting with the spinning reel is far easier than with the revolving spool reel, although it is not nearly so accurate when it comes to plunking the bait in an exact spot. You can get close with the spinning tackle, but you won't hit the "nail on the head" as consistently as with the conventional rig. Use of the conventional reel calls for educated thumb control. With the spinning reel, line peels off a stationary spool. But when using the conventional reel, the line comes off a revolving spool that accelerates from zero to tremendous speed immediately after the thumb is lifted from it on the casting stroke.

Many conventional reels come with anti-backlash devices that help but don't completely eliminate use of the thumb. The fisherman must still use thumb pressure on the spool to keep it from revolving faster than line pays out. If he doesn't, he is certain to end up with a backlash or "bird's nest" of tangled line on the spool. If the backlash occurs when the sinker is still heading out to sea at high speed, the resulting tangle may stop the sinker's forward momentum so abruptly as to at least snap baits off the hook. The force of the shock may also be so sudden as to pop off the sinker or the entire terminal rig.

In the days when linen line was popular for surf fishing, the old salts always wetted the line on the spool before casting. They did this to prevent the friction from the rapidly moving line from burning their thumbs. This can still be done with braided synthetic line since this type of line will pick up a little moisture. It won't work with monofilament as it picks up no moisture whatsoever. Therefore a fellow with a tender thumb may want to use a thumb stall or tab to protect the skin. Use of a stall or tab, however, gives the fisherman less sensitive control over the speed of the revolving spool. Some fishermen apply thumb pressure to the side of the reel spool that is an unchanging surface. If the thumb is applied to the line proper on the spool, the surface will be ever changing as the diameter of the remaining line on the spool decreases as line pays out. Indeed, an educated thumb is needed for this situation.

16
Special Tricks

Regardless of the fish species involved, there are always a few special tricks that can be used to improve one's fishing odds.

One of the most successful is the fish-finder rig, which can be used in all aspects of channel bass fishing. It is a particularly good rig to use in the surf and around jetties, and it is a type of rig that allows the fisherman to use the currents to his advantage.

The fish-finder rig is one in which the line is allowed to run freely through the eye of the sinker. In operation the sinker holds fast in one spot on the bottom, but since the fishing line runs freely through the sinker eye, the current is able to sweep the baited hook over a wide area. When fishing this type of rig, the reel is usually left in free spool to allow the line to pay out slowly with the current. This rig has a distinct advantage in channel bass fishing because of the fish's habit of nosing and mouthing baits. When line starts paying out at a steady clip, the fisherman knows a fish has taken the bait. He can then engage the reel gears and strike to drive the hook home.

The fish-finder rig is most effective when fish are not plentiful, since this is when channel bass are most wary about taking baits. If the fish are plentiful or in schools, they are not apt to toy with the bait. The competition for food will make them grab a bait and take off.

Plastic lined sleeves with a ring eye are made expressly for the fish-finder rig. The fishing line is run through the sleeve and then tied to a barrel swivel that in turn is connected to the leader. Then by means of a snap or connecting link, the sinker is attached to the ring eye on the sleeve. An alternate method is to attach the sinker to the end of the line, and then connect the leader to the line above the sinker. A connecting link is used for this purpose.

A different sort of fish-finder rig can be made with a cork or plastic float. The line is run through the hole that runs lengthwise in the float, and then a small knot is tied in the line at some point above the float. The depth of the water will determine where the knot is tied. The line will run through the float until the knot strikes the hole. The float is allowed to drift along in the current with the bait suspended a short distance off the bottom. This rig is excellent for fishing over bottoms covered with rocks and snags. Since the float can slip freely up and down the line between the swivel at the leader and the knot in the line, the rig is popularly called the "slip cork."

When casting out in all of the "slip" methods described, the sinker or float is forced against the swivel that connects to the leader. Therefore use a swivel large enough so that it will not wedge into the hole in either the sleeve or the float.

Another special trick is the surf chum cage. It is just like chumming from a boat, except in the surf the chum cage is anchored to the bottom, whereas in boat fishing the chum bag is suspended from the stern of the boat.

As far as I know, there are no commercially marketed surf chum cages. So if the fisherman wants to use one, he will have to build it himself. It isn't a major construction job.

Construct a box frame about a foot square. Use iron building rods and weld the corners and joints so it will withstand the pounding of the surf. Then cover the entire box with half-inch mesh chicken wire. Don't use wire screening because it is too fine. You want small enough mesh to keep the large chunks of chum in the box but still large enough to permit tiny portions of chum to carry out with the current.

The bottom of the box should have two iron strips about four inches wide welded in the form of an X. These iron strips coupled with the weight of the building rods will be sufficient to anchor the box in place in the surf. If additional weight is needed, a brick can be put inside.

The X on the bottom will keep the box from digging into the

sand and sinking out of sight. And, of course, a trap door will be needed at the top to facilitate putting in or removing chum. The chum itself is made up of chunks of bait fish, crabs broken in half, and other forms of marine life that may be available to the fisherman.

On high tide the box should be anchored in the first trough off the beach. On lower tides the fisherman may have to wade out to the second or third trough. Be sure to attach a float with a long line to the box. This will enable the fisherman to locate the box when he quits fishing, and it will also serve to let the fisherman know if the chum box is being moved either by the breakers or current action.

Bits of marine life and fish oils will fan out from the chum and carry with the current to form a slick that can be effective at quite some distance. The fisherman then casts his baited hooks into the water where the chum slick carries. If he sets out three or four rigs, one should be cast out up-current from the chum box. The reason is to have a baited hook in an area for those fish that may follow the chum slick in and then keep moving up-current past the box.

The drawback to chum box fishing is that the slick will attract a wide variety of fish. So in order to keep from losing bait to a lot of unwanted species, the fisherman should use baits that are difficult to tear from the hook. In this case, squid and mullet are the best choice. Menhaden makes the ideal chum, and because it is fatty and quite oily it leaves a wide slick that is effective over a long distance. Menhaden should never be put in the box whole. Cut them in chunks so the fats and oils can drain out easily.

Years ago I saw a couple of fellows scoop up dime-size shells off a Texas beach and fill two bushel baskets. Then they waded out into the first off-beach trough where the water was about waist deep and dumped the stuff all in one spot. I thought they were nuts. But when they started to fish right in the area where they had dumped the shells, I walked over and started to ask questions.

They were seeking redfish, and they explained that they had picked up shells in which there was still live marine life. They went on to explain that when cleaning redfish they often found this same shell life in the stomachs of the fish. It was their way of baiting up the water. They pointed out that it only worked if the surf was light and there were little or no currents. If the surf was breaking heavy, it would quickly wash the shell life back to the beach.

They had to know what they were talking about because inside of an hour they caught a pair of 12-pound redfish from the area they had "shelled." Meanwhile I was fishing some 200 yards further down the beach and caught nothing. Over the years I have seen other fishermen use the same trick and noted that most of them got results.

It is not a very sporting way to fish, but if a fellow is after a mess of fish, particularly rat reds back in the shallow bays, there is the old-fashioned trotline. It can be used with cut bait, live bait, or artificial lures. The lures, however, can be used only if currents are running. The lures should be sinkers or underwater runners. Rig the trotline high enough so the lures won't touch bottom to foul their action. The current will make them wiggle enticingly.

The same method with the same baits can be used in the surf by rigging the trotline so it diagonally crosses a trough. It will catch fish, but as I stated earlier there is no sport to it.

A heavy surf sinker can often rob a fish—even a big fish—of some of its sporting fight. If the sinker could be released, the fisherman would get a lot more sport out of his game. Well, the sinker can be released if it is attached above the leader. Simply make a loop in the line and keep it in place by tying a piece of light test line across it. The sinker rides on this piece of light test line. When a big fish is on, the strain will pop the light line and release the sinker, and then the fisherman can fight a fish that isn't encumbered by a heavy surf sinker. The fisherman using this trick should use inexpensive sinkers, for he can expect to lose a lot of them. Remember some of the sinkers will be lost on a heavy strike even though the hook doesn't bed in the fish's mouth.

17
Tackle Care

The initial outlay for the proper tackle for channel bass fishing is most reasonable. It can, however, become expensive if the fisherman fails to keep the gear clean and in good condition. Regardless the claims made by some tackle manufacturers, tackle is not self protective against damage from the elements. Any article that gets wet is subject to rust or mildew. This is further complicated in salt-water fishing since the addition of salt promotes corrosion, which can be even more of a headache than rust.

Rust is easy to see; corrosion is not. Corrosion can freeze ferrules together, lock the screw rings on reel seats, pit metal parts, and completely eat out delicate metal fittings. For instance, a reel that has salt-water exposure and then is stored uncleaned in a damp place can be completely ruined in a month. Corrosion attack isn't limited to reels. It attacks with equal vigor hooks, swivels and snaps, lures, metal fittings on rods, and the fittings on tackle boxes.

The tackle that requires the most cleaning and upkeep will be the fisherman's reels because of their many working parts. The least amount of cleaning will be after bay, jetty, pier, and boat trips. Here the work will be mainly that of a thorough washing to remove all traces of salt. Then dry the reel and lightly oil the working metal parts, exercising care in keeping oil off the drag. Oil or grease that gets on drag parts, especially if they are made of fiber as many of them are today, can cause the drag to slip or bind. The reel should be stored in a dust-proof container— the plastic bag bread comes in is good—in a dry place.

If the reel has been used for surf fishing, cleaning becomes more of a chore. You have both salt and sand to contend with. No fisherman in his right mind is going to lay an expensive reel on the sand, but there is always the possibility of accidentally dropping it. Even if the reel never gets closer than three feet to the beach sand, it is certain to pick up sand in its working parts. The sand can be blown on it by the wind or it can be picked up by the line itself. Consequently the care for a reel used in surf fishing requires more than just a rinsing in fresh water. To do the job properly it should be dismantled so that inner working parts can be reached. Wash thoroughly and then grease lightly. If it is necessary to use something stronger than soapy water to remove old grease infested with sand or salt, try white gasoline or kerosene. Don't use carbon tetrachloride for it may dissolve plastic parts on the reel.

When disassembling a reel lay the parts out in a line in the order in which they are removed, and then when putting it back together, start with the last part and work backwards down the line. Run several strips of scotch tape across the table and stick all parts to the tape. It beats hunting for them on the floor. When reassembling the reel, don't force parts. Keep turning them around until they slip easily into place. Tighten screws down to hold but never over-tighten. These screws have comparatively soft threads that can be stripped by over-tightening. A tiny drop of oil in screw holes will prevent the fittings from corroding and freezing up. When a new reel is purchased, a reel tool that is a combination screw driver and wrench comes in the box. Use this tool. The screwdriver head is made to fit the screw head slots, and the wrench holes are the exact size for nut fittings. The fellow who uses the garden variety screwdriver and pliers in lieu of a wrench runs the risk of twisting off screw heads and badly scarring nuts. The wrong tools can make a reel's appearance age years in a single night.

Rods require far less upkeep than reels. For the most part they can be kept serviceable by washing in fresh water, drying, and then storing in a dry place at room temperature. Never store a rod in a place subject to high temperature. If the rod is leaned against a wall and then subjected to appreciable heat for a long period, it will take a set or bend. The closet that houses the household hot-water heater may be dry, but it is the worst place in the world to store any fishing rod. The heat is enough to put a set in a glass rod. On a split bamboo rod this same heat will cause the glue to let go and the blanks to separate.

Always check rod windings. Unless badly frayed, they can be repaired with a coat of rod varnish. If the rod tip is grooved, remove it and replace with a new one. Monofilament line is very hard, and constant running in and out of line on the same spot can wear a groove in the metal of the tip top. This groove can become just sharp enough to cut the line at the wrong time.

Sectional rods should be completely taken down. Clean and dry both the male and female ferrules and wipe with a fine film of oil when putting the rod up for storage. The rod should be stored disassembled. An important point to remember is to wipe all the oil off the ferrules before assembling the rod to use again. If you don't, the sections will stick and will be hard to separate again. To make an easy fit when assembling, run the male ferrule through your hair or alongside your nose. It will pick up just enough lubrication to prevent binding.

When the ferrules on jointed rods stick, don't attempt to use undue force or twisting to free them. Often the heat from a match flame will be sufficient to make the metal expand just enough to allow separation. Rod ferrules stick because of foreign matter or surface scratches that bind against the surface of the opposite ferrule. These scratches are the result of inadequate cleaning and poor storage. Resist the temptation to remove the scratches with a fine file. This may be a quick way, but it will only damage the ferrule and make for an even poorer fit. It may require an hour's work, but the proper way is to polish off the scratch with a cloth dipped in extra fine grade valve-grinding compound.

Check ring screw lock reel seats carefully. Wash off any salt and sand that may collect. Clean the spiral grooves with a fine screwdriver or steel wool. Then coat with a fine film of grease and run the tightening screw ring up and down the shaft several times to distribute the grease well into the grooves. Never use lubricating oil because it runs too much when wet and then dries out to a dirty sludge.

Back in the days when linen line was popular, their upkeep used to be murder. The stuff had to be washed thoroughly, stretched out to dry, and then re-spooled on the reel. Most of this work has been eliminated by today's synthetic lines. Unless used in surf fishing, where the lines are likely to pick up sand, they don't even have to be washed after every trip. There is absolutely no need to stretch the line out to dry. When spooling it back on the reel, just pass the free end through a bath towel, and this will pick up all the moisture. The line should be checked for fraying, for such spots are a sign of weakness. Usually this fraying will be found in the last three feet of line. This is the part that in fishing is likely to be scraped against sharp rocks, pilings, etc. Especially after a long day of hard casting, the standing end of the line that bites against the rod tip top on each cast is likely to be frayed. It is a good idea to cut off and throw away a yard of line after each trip. It's not being wasteful; it's just good insurance. Look at it this way. If you have 250 yards of line on the spool, you can cut off a yard after each of 25 trips and still have 225 yards on the spool. The average fisherman makes about a dozen trips a year, so he can still get two year's use out of the line.

Terminal tackle, too, needs care. Wash and dry hooks and keep them in an air-tight container. You might even line the bottom of the container with a rag dipped in fish oil as extra protection against rust and corrosion. But never put machine oil on the rag, as this type of oil is foreign to fish and will repel them. Fish oil, on the other hand, helps to attract fish. Show the same care to swivels, snaps, and other types of hardware used for terminal tackle. Lures should be washed and dried before storage.

Oil the working parts of the tackle box and keep the interior dry and free of rust, salt, and sand. It is a good idea to occasionally open the box and allow it to air in the sun.

Never use sandpaper to remove rust or corrosion, otherwise metal surfaces will be marred and scratched. If the deposits are heavy, rub lightly with fine steel wool. Then follow this up with a cloth dipped in extra fine valve-grinding compound. This two-step operation will polish the metal back to its original shine without scarring the surface.

Metal sand spikes are best protected from the elements by coating them with rust-inhibiting paint. Any working or screw parts on the sand spike should be coated with grease. Wash gaff

Channel bass have a tendency to work parallel to jetties. This aerial photo was taken during the height of redfish run at Bolivar, Texas, North Jetty.

When this jetty was built, the rocks were laid evenly. Walking is no problem except at night or when waves wash over the rocks.

Boat cuts through jetties are excellent places to seek channel bass. Converging currents sweep baitfish away from the protection of the rocks.

Piers do a land office business when redfish move into the surf. This is part of a crowd on a Texas pier during the height of a fall run.

When the channel bass are running, big fish like this are commonly caught from the piers.

A large landing net is a good way to secure big redfish when fishing from piers. The net is dropped into the water. The fish is worked up to the pier, led over the net, and then swiftly lifted aboard. (Photo courtesy Howard Robbins)

Piers offer many shots at channel bass. When the fish are out deep, the place to fish is from the seaward T-head. Spots along the length of the pier are the choice places when the fish move into shallow water.

A nice catch of redfish off a Chandeleur Island beach some 100 miles east of New Orleans. Angler in foreground is working hook out of fish's mouth, while another fisherman in background battles still another channel bass. (Photo courtesy Louisiana Tourist Development Commission)

Big channel bass like this do not fight near the surface or put on aerial display like tarpon and sailfish. Reds fight down deep with many pulsating runs.

Surf casting is an art of good coordination. Here the author is preparing to cast with surf spinning tackle.

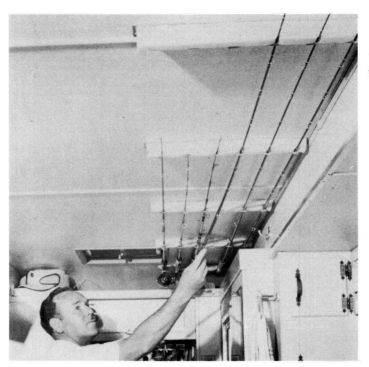

This is an ideal way to store rods to prevent them from taking a set.
This Eaz-lift Rod-Rac can be installed in a camper, trailer, or home.

Channel bass in the 6- to 12-pound class often mass in dense schools.
Texas fishermen Bo Collins and Robert Dee had a real chore on their
hands dressing out 97 such fish caught on a single t¨

Channel bass this size are edible. They are too coarse for frying but make good table fare when baked or cooked in a chowder.

This channel bass weighed almost 50 pounds. It was fun to catch, but fish this large make poor table fare. They are suitable mainly for chowder. A channel bass this size is a breeder, and unless desired for food or mounting, it should be returned unharmed to the water.

This 44¼-pound channel bass caught by R. E. Robison of Galveston, Texas, set a spinning record for 10-pound test line in 1961.

hooks and check points for sharpness. A dull gaff hook is hard to drive through the scales of a big channel bass. Always thoroughly wash landing nets, using extra care to see that all fish slime and blood is removed from the netting. If you leave this matter on, the netting is certain to rot.

18

Edibility

A few days before I started to write this chapter, one of the boys
in *The Galveston Daily News'* composing room dropped by my
desk with a request. He wanted me to list his name with his catch
in my daily fishing report. He was quite proud of the 35-pound
channel bass he had caught from the surf that previous night. I
didn't blame him. A fish that size is nothing to be sneezed at.

Then he made a remark that caused me to frown. "I'm going
to get all the boys together and have a big fish fry," he said. He
saw the frown on my face and added: "Oh, you'll be invited.
I'll have it on a night when you're off."

I hastened to explain to him that that was not what I had in
mind. "I would be glad to come," I remarked, "but don't save
any fish for me. The meat from those big reds is poor, and personally I wouldn't eat a big one unless it was used in fish chowder
or I was on the verge of starvation. I really think you ought to
try eating some of that fish yourself before you go around inviting
the buddies in."

A few days later he dropped by my desk again. This time he
said: "I took your advice. My wife fixed some of that fish in a
chowder yesterday and it was fair. I also had her fry up a couple
of pieces. That fried stuff was lousy. It was stringy, tough, and
tasteless. And I always thought redfish was choice eating."

For the information of all concerned, the channel bass or redfish is choice eating as long as you pick the right size fish. If you
like it fried, then stick with fish less than three pounds; those
running four to 12 are fine for baking. Anything over that is suitable only for fish chowder, where the chunks of meat can be

tenderized, flavored, and made juicy with various other ingredients. The difference in table fare between the three- or four-pound rat red and the 40-pound bull is the same as that between the yearling and the 20-year-old steer.

So with those big ones, unless you figure on having the fish prepared in a chowder or mounting it, the best thing to do is to release it so it can live and fight again another day. The fish is far too grand a warrior to end up wrapped in paper and dumped in the garbage can or left to rot on the beach. A few of our states quite sensibly have possession limits on big channel bass. These regulations help to cut down on wasted game and aid in protecting brood stock.

Small reds are best when prepared fresh. The meat is white, firm, and tasty. If the fisherman brings in too many fish for a family meal, the surplus fish can be frozen and stored for weeks. But when thawed out, the flesh won't be quite so firm and some of the flavor will be lost. How much flavor is lost will depend upon how well the fish is prepared before it is placed in the freezer.

All entrails should be removed and the body cavity should be washed thoroughly in running cold water. Never allow the fish to soak. Remove the head, all gills, and tail and cut away the fins. You can freeze the fish with or without scales. Personally I prefer to freeze them with the scales left on, for they are tough and they help to protect the meat from freezer "burn." Also, the scales come off much easier after a frozen fish has been thawed out than they do off a freshly caught fish.

Small fish—one- and two-pounders—can be fried whole or filleted. The fisherman will need a pair of two-pounders to make a meal for a family of four. Remember the weight loss in dressing out a channel bass is approximately 30 percent. If the fish is filleted, the loss is closer to 40 percent.

In baking larger channel bass the flavor can be improved considerably by preparing a dressing and stuffing the cavity. An oyster stuffing in a baked redfish can make for a real tasty dish.

Big bulls, especially those running in excess of thirty pounds, are brutes to prepare. You'll need a saw or hatchet to remove the head and gills. Scaling, too, is a mean job. Many times I have nailed a big red by its tail to a tree and then knocked off the scales with a hatchet or meat cleaver. It's just as tough to skin a big one, too, for the skin doesn't pull off the meat like a glove.

After the fish has been gutted, headed, and tailed, the best procedure to follow is to cut off steaks about three inches thick. Then with a sharp paring knife, the skin can be removed and the meat trimmed off the bones.

Freezing does absolutely nothing toward improving the flavor or quality of meat from a big channel bass. It may help to tenderize the meat, but whether it is fresh or frozen a week or six months, it will still taste something like dry cotton. It can be improved upon by baking and a lot of basting with a tasty sauce. But flesh from a thirty-pound red runs a very poor second to the baked ten- or twelve-pounder.

By far the best way to prepare a big channel bass for the table is to get your wife to agree to a day in the kitchen. Then with huge pots prepare a mammoth chowder. True, you won't be able to eat it all in a day, but it will keep very nicely frozen in quart containers. When thawed out and allowed to simmer for several hours over a low fire, the large chunks of meat will break down into many small pieces. This doesn't hurt a bit, and only adds to the flavor.

One other point about the chowder. If you like potatoes mixed in, don't prepare them in the original chowder to be frozen. You will find that when cooked potatoes are frozen they turn to mush. It is far better to prepare the potatoes on the day you plan to eat the chowder. Dump them in the chowder and let the whole works simmer for about a half hour before serving. The potatoes will be tender but not mushy.

The fisherman dressing out a big channel bass is likely to run into something that may upset him. When he bones flesh away from the backbone, he may get a shock in seeing small worms in the flesh next to the bone. This can upset a tyro enough to make him throw the whole fish away. There is really no need for this. Even if the worms are left in the meat, they are not harmful to humans after the flesh is cooked.

At various times of the year these same parasitic worms are found in most all species of large fish. Let me repeat they in no way contaminate the meat. They just look unpleasant.

19

Regulations

Sport fishing regulations pertaining to channel bass vary from state to state, and the fisherman who chooses to vagabond in quest of these fish should study the laws. Enforcement is strict and violators can find it costly. Fortunately for the sports fisherman, regulations are far less restrictive and complicated than those pertaining to commercial fishermen taking the same fish.

Some states have channel bass regulations that the sportsman must observe. Others have none where strict sports fishing is concerned. However, the trend in recent years has been one of leaning more and more to channel bass regulations that affect the sportsman. Marine biologists are truly concerned about this fish. Its range isn't as extensive as it used to be, and in some quarters there is talk that the fish overall are not as plentiful as in former years. The fish's former range into state waters north of Virginia most certainly has been affected by pollution, urban shoreline developments, and a change in the marine bottom ecology. These same factors are likely to change channel bass habits and population in still plentiful areas in decades to come unless major steps are taken to curb estuarine pollution.

It is important to note that the channel bass isn't the only fish that is having its range altered. Consider the Atlantic salmon, which in some circles is being viewed as a vanishing species. It is interesting to note that ranges where the channel bass once roamed in number are highly industrialized, and where there is industry there is the by-product of waste. For a long time in this nation, waste was simply permitted to run untreated into estuarine complexes on the theory that it would eventually dilute to the point of being non-toxic.

Events in recent years have proven otherwise. While the process of dilution may have rendered the waste non-toxic and harmless to man, it hasn't been sufficient to insure stable habitat for marine life. Consequently the complexes that once were major marine spawning grounds have been turned into virtual deserts barely able to support any marine life.

Remedial measures are underway to see that sewerage, industrial, and chemical waste are sufficiently treated before they are released into the sea. It is a question now of whether the measures were started in time. The marine ecology, which slowly developed over thousands of years, may never recover.

A matter of great concern to marine biologists—and sports fishermen should be equally concerned—is the breeding habit of the channel bass. These fish normally don't spawn until they are three to four years of age and in excess of 30 to 32 inches in length. Therefore a number of states prohibit the taking of big channel bass for commercial purposes.

Regulations in Texas, for example, prohibit the sale of channel bass in excess of 32 inches long, head off, or 35 inches long, head on. Sportsmen, however, can catch and keep fish in excess of these sizes. There is no bag limit on the number of big channel bass a sports fisherman can catch and keep in Lone Star State waters. The only Texas regulation that governs the channel bass angler is one pertaining to minimum length. It is illegal to keep reds under 14 inches in length. This regulation is on the books in order to protect the fish so they have a reasonably good chance to reach maturity to spawn. Until reds are about 18 inches long, they spend much of their time in bays where they fall easy prey to fishermen.

Still other states have regulations on how many big channel bass a sportsman can retain. For example, in Virginia waters a sportsman is limited to two channel bass, 32 inches in length or longer. The measurement is from tip of nose to tip of tail. This is the daily possession limit in Virginia. The regulation is a good one, and one that the writer hopes all states will eventually adopt. I have seen far too many large channel bass end up on the garbage heap to feel otherwise about the matter. There is no place for the "game hog" in either fishing or hunting. The supply is not inexhaustible. Like Texas, the state of Virginia also has a minimum length, 12 inches, for channel bass to be keepers.

A license for fishing in salt water is required in some states; others have none. Texas has what it calls a universal fishing license that sells for $2.15. It is required of residents as well as non-residents in any fresh water or salt water within or bordering the state if the fisherman uses any type of reel device. Some states require the fisherman to have a valid license in his possession if he fishes with artificial lures.

Actually licenses, including the non-resident types, are inexpensive. If the fisherman goes for the small reds that frequently meander up bayous, creeks, and rivers, it would be smart to have a license. The fisherman's views of how far salt water goes up the creek might be different from the views of the apprehending game warden. I have seen this happen a number of times, and in most cases where non-resident fishermen were involved, the judge made the fine stick.

It's just wise to play it safe and buy a license. True sportsmen know a license is money well spent. These funds go a long way toward studies of ways and means of protecting our game and fish heritage for centuries to come. Resident licenses are good for a year and non-resident licenses can be obtained on a year basis or for short vacation periods of a few days. All states have requirements necessary to qualify for a resident license. Usually this period is six months residence immediately prior to application for license. States also have exemptions pertaining to age, and some states have special exemptions for military service personnel. These, however, should be checked in the game and fish digests of each state in which a fellow plans to fish, since there is a great deal of variation from state to state.

Following are the prices of licenses in states that still come within the plentiful range of channel bass.

Alabama—Resident: annual $2; non-resident: annual $5, seven consecutive days $2.

Florida—Resident: annual $2; non-resident: annual statewide

$8, 14 consecutive days $3.25, five consecutive days $2.25.

Georgia—Resident: annual $1.25; non-resident: annual $6.25, three consecutive days $1.25.

Louisiana—Resident: $1; non-resident: annual $5, seven consecutive days $2.

Mississippi—Resident: annual $3; non-resident: annual $6, tourist three days $1.

North Carolina—Resident: annual $4.25; non-resident: annual $8.25, five consecutive days $3.75, one day $1.65.

South Carolina—Resident: annual $1.10; non-resident: annual $10.25, ten consecutive days $3.10.

Texas—Resident: annual $2.15; non-resident: annual $2.15.

Virginia—Resident: annual $2.15; non-resident: annual $3.50.

20

The Right Clothes

Don't ever let anyone kid you about dressing for fishing, for when it comes to some phases of channel bass fishing, there are the right and wrong clothes to wear. What you wear can have a lot to do with the amount of luck you have with fish.

Whether you are fishing from a boat or pier, dress doesn't make a lot of difference as long as it is comfortable and protective for the type of weather that prevails. It's a different story when you go in for surf or bay fishing and when wading the shallow flats.

A yachting cap and duck white may fit the picture in boating circles, but this wear will only get you laughs and few fish when it comes to working the surf and bays. The fisherman must always take into consideration that channel bass are wary and easy to spook. If the fish can see you, chances are excellent that it will hightail out of the area.

Surf wear should be loose and comfortable. You are bound to get wet when fishing the surf, so avoid wearing close-fitting clothes since they have a tendency to dry slowly. Wet clothes and a brisk wind, especially at night, can make life pretty uncomfortable. If you can drive your car on the beach, it is a good idea to take along a change of clothing. If the weather is quite warm, wear khaki pants for wading out into the surf. These pants fit loose and the material dries quite fast in the warm sun and breeze. Swimming trunks are okay for areas in which there are no submerged rocks. But if there are rocks in the area, the khaki pants will offer some protection against scratches and cuts should you slip and fall.

105

In cold weather go with chest-high waders. They will allow you to wade out a good distance without getting wet. Hip boots are good for going out only about knee deep. Remember rolling surf will strike your legs and the spray can wet you up to the waist, which can be most uncomfortable in fall and winter temperatures.

Chest-high waders are a poor choice in hot weather for you can get soaking wet from sweat. Some sort of shoes should be worn, even on sandy beaches, to protect your feet from small but sharp shells. Wading sandals or sneakers are ideal. All clothing should be drab in color so as not to reflect light.

Those chest-high waders are the best choice for wading bay flats in cool weather, for they come up high enough to protect you from wind-whipped spray. In warm weather cotton pants and sneakers will suffice. Drab-colored clothing is far more important in bay fishing than in the surf. Keep in mind that in bay fishing you will be much closer to the fish, and if the sun is bright, light-colored clothes will reflect a lot of light. Regardless what color clothes the fisherman wears, he should always try to fish facing into the sun in early morning and late afternoon. A sun behind him may cast long enough shadows on the water to spook the fish. In this respect a long-billed cap and sunglasses or Polaroid glasses are great. I prefer Polaroid for they will reduce glare and permit a certain amount of vision down into the water.

Protective eye wear is a must when it comes to fishing the surf. Even on an overcast day the glare bouncing off breaking waves can be fierce. If a fellow is fair-skinned, he should apply suntan lotion to exposed parts of his body as protection against sun and wind burn. Protective eye wear and suntan lotion are necessary when it comes to fishing from jetties, piers, and boats.

If the bay fisherman uses a boat, its sides should be painted in some subdued color. White may look clean and wholesome, but it sure can reflect a lot of light and be seen from a considerable distance. The white sides of a boat in shallow water may be just enough to keep the fish out of casting range.

Considerable care is necessary for certain articles of clothing. Shoes, whether they are sneakers or wading sandals, should be washed in fresh water and then dried thoroughly before storage in order to prevent rot and mildew.

Waders and boots require somewhat different care. Rinse them off thoroughly in fresh water. Any scum, oil, or grease that may get on them should be removed with soapy water. Oil and grease are natural enemies of rubber. When drying waders and boots, dry them carefully inside and out and then store them in a cool, dry place. If they are made of rubber, don't fold or roll them tightly for this can cause the rubber to develop hairline cracks that in turn will become miserable leaks. Rubber waders and boots can be repaired with light inner-tube patches, or with repair material furnished by the product manufacturer.

Many waders and boots today are made of plastic or synthetic materials that require remarkably little upkeep. I prefer the plastics over rubber because of the lighter weight. However, the plastics and synthetics should still be washed free of salt, scum, oil, and grease. These garments are easy to repair with materials that come with them at the time of purchase. Like their rubber counterparts they should be stored in a cool, dry place. Avoid folding or rolling tightly, for if the temperature in the storage place drops considerably, the plastic has a tendency to harden and become brittle.

The best way to store waders and boots—rubber, plastic, or synthetic—is to stuff them loosely with newspaper and then hang them upside down. In this way there will be no creases to harden into cracks that later might become leaks. Proper storage of this gear can make it last for years.

21
Big Red Adventures

Episodes with big red have provided me with some wild out-
doors adventures, and when I look back on some of them, I
realize that indeed someone up there must have been watching
over me.

Two really close ones occurred in 1944 when I was in the
Army and stationed at Fort Crockett, a harbor defense command
base guarding the sea approaches to Galveston. The outfit I
was in was made up completely of limited service personnel—
men too blind, too crippled or too old to be trusted to go out
to shoot at the enemy, yet men capable enough to man such
war-winning departments like post headquarters, public rela-
tions, special services, motor pools and the like.

The fact that we were misfits in an army of 1-As limited the
whole bunch in the matter of promotions, a source of unending
gripes. Still "limited service" on our records had its advantages,
one being mass exodus from the post on weekends to pursue
various forms of recreation, some not exactly approved in Vic-
torian circles.

It so happened that our company commander, Captain Hayes
Spellman, a motor pool sergeant whose name I can't recall, and
myself were avid fishermen. And almost every weekend the
captain took off his bars and we commandeered a jeep and
took off for the Galveston South Jetty. The area was strictly
off limits to all personnel except those carrying special passes.
The captain had no trouble with passes. All he had to do was
write them out himself. The motor pool sergeant was a member
in good standing in the trio because he could get transportation

any time. And I mean any time. I was sort of special, too, being in special services and in charge of checking out sports and recreational equipment to post personnel. Certain fishing gear was earmarked and never checked out to anyone who was not a member of our trio. Extra gear was also stacked in a hidden corner to take care of any special guests we might desire to take along on the trips.

The first wild trip took place on an October morning during the height of the annual surf run of channel bass. To reach the jetty we had to drive down the beach and pass on the bullet side of an infiltration course, where every Saturday morning new draftees—more limited service men—were given a taste of life under zipping bullets. Our captain had to pull rank on a second lieutenant to get him to hold up firing so we could pass. We got the usual undercover help from the range sergeant, who backed our captain to the hilt that we had official inspection business at the jetty. The range sergeant, who lived off the post with his family, was always rewarded with fresh fish.

When we got to the jetty, the topping was being combed repeatedly by waves washing across. So we elected to fish from the beach. After an hour or so of nothing, we decided to chance walking out on the dangerous topping. Slipping, sliding, and at times crawling, we got out about a quarter of a mile. It was no easy job when white water, sometimes knee deep, raced across the topping. The water was perhaps 10 to 15 feet deep on each side of the jetty, and had any of us washed overboard, it certainly would have been the end. At the time all we had on our minds were fish.

We got into the wildest redfish action I have ever experienced and almost every cast resulted in a redfish. All were uniform in size, 10 to 12 pounds. When we quit, we had 60 odd fish. Fortunately the motor pool sergeant had brought along a long length of rope. A movie of us dragging those fish back to shore would have made a great comedy piece. Sometimes we could drag the fish along right on the topping. Then a wave would wash them over the side and down into the rocks. And what a job it was getting that load of fish back up. By the time we got back to the jeep most of the fish were pretty well scaled from being dragged over the rough rocks and barnacles.

We couldn't get all the fish into the jeep, so the captain designated me to stay with them while he and the sergeant drove some ten miles back to the post to get a larger vehicle. It really didn't take long, but since I was soaking wet, it seemed like hours in that cold October wind.

The range sergeant was, of course, rewarded with a half dozen fish. The remainder ended up in our company mess and our outfit had a hell of a fish dinner and beer bust Sunday night.

A week later we—the same trio—almost got into serious trouble again. This time in the same area. The water was even rougher than it had been a week earlier, so we decided to cross a small slue that ran between the jetty and a huge sandbar on the ship channel side. We crossed at low tide. The slue was about a hundred feet wide and three feet deep. Again we got into channel bass fishing like mad and caught several dozen ranging up to 25 or 30 pounds. Meanwhile the tide had started in and when we quit fishing the water had risen about a foot.

We dragged our fish across the sand flat and found the little hundred-foot slue had expanded to around 200 feet wide and resembled a racing river as the tide and current flowed through. I was the first one to start across. The first 150 feet weren't bad at all. The water was about chest deep. And then—chung! I stepped out of sight. When I came up and managed to dog-paddle back to shallow water, I saw my helmet liner swiftly drifting down current.

After doing some probing with the fishing rods, we discovered the racing current had dug out a deep channel between the sandbar and rocks. We figured it was around six or seven feet deep, and how that tide was racing through it. Since I was the strongest swimmer, I was nominated to peel down to Olympic wear to swim across. It was an easy swim, although I got scratched up quite a bit climbing up the rocks on the jetty side. I swam over pulling the line off one of the fishing rods. Then the other fellows tied the line to the long rope we carried, and I pulled our fish across. They pulled the rope back with another line, and on the next trip I hauled over the rods and reel and my clothes. Then the rope went back and I pulled the captain over. The sergeant brought up the rear.

An hour later, the entire sandbar on which we had been

fishing was under a foot of water. I don't do nutty things like that any more. I check areas carefully and always make sure there is a safe avenue of retreat. The same waters we fished that day have in the years since claimed the lives of at least a dozen fishermen. They got into trouble as we had, but we were lucky and somebody upstairs was watching over us. I do believe God watches over fools and drunks. And that day we were fools.

Another memorable redfish haul took place in, of all places, a duck blind on the flats in Copano Bay on the middle Texas coast. My host was one who always carried a couple of rods and reels in his boat at all times. We had the boat tied securely inside the blind and were all set for some fancy redhead—ducks, that is—shooting. The ducks were as thick as mosquitoes, but unfortunately for us, the fog was thicker than that proverbial pea soup. We could barely see the decoys and they were only about 25 yards out from the blind. Although the redheads wouldn't decoy, they flew all around, but you can't shoot what you can't see. All we could hear were whirring wings.

Then my host noticed Vs all around on the surface of the water. It didn't take long to recognize the source of the Vs was a huge school of redfish. We found a long dead mullet on the bottom of the boat and cut it into bait, broke out the fishing tackle, and started catching redfish. It was one of the few times in my life that I have seen redfish feed with such reckless abandon. By all the rules of good channel bass fishing, we should have spooked those fish to the next county. We made noise casting, bumping the bottom and sides of the boat, and laughing and talking quite loud. When we ran out of mullet, we simply diced up one of the redfish for additional bait and went on catching fish. We ended the morning with something like four dozen reds running three to five pounds in size. We didn't fire a cap at the ducks that day.

The next two days, however, the fog was gone and so were the redfish. But the redhead ducks were still around and we got our limits with no sweat.

I suppose the single catch that stands out most vividly was a 41-pounder caught in 1960. It occurred in July and at a time when bull channel bass normally don't range into the shallow

Texas surf. At the time I was casting a yellow leadhead jig for speckled trout. I was using a whippy seven-foot rod with an open-face reel loaded with 200 yards of ten-pound test line.

I had been casting for about an hour, and in that time I picked up two or three medium-size specks. Then I had a solid strike and the fish in its initial run must have peeled off 30 or 40 yards of line. Then the fish sulked and right away I figured I had a big jackfish. I don't care for jacks, and usually when I hook one I just snub off and break the line. But this time I thought it would be fun to play the fish on the light tackle.

At the time I was standing in waist-deep water and about a hundred yards from a beachfront fishing pier. The fish made two more runs in the direction of the pier, and shortly I was about 50 feet from the pilings. Folks on the pier gathered to watch, and one yelled down asking what I had on, and I replied it was probably a big jackfish.

The water was slick calm and very clear, just right for speckled trout fishing. Some of the folks on the pier shouted down that they could see my fish. Then one old salt on the pier put down his rod and reel and shouted down:

"Jackfish, hell! Bub, you gotta big redfish on! I can see the spot on his tail when he rolls."

It came as a shock. And I changed quickly from an attitude of fun and games to one of dead serious fishing. I checked the drag and noted the remaining line on the reel spool, guessing I had about a hundred yards left. Luck was with me. The fish must have seen the pier pilings for it changed directions 180 degrees. That was a real break. Had the fish gone under the pier, I most certainly would have lost it.

The fish made a number of runs. How many I don't know. Fortunately the runs were parallel to the beach. That is all but one, which gave me some trying moments. That run was to seaward and line melted off the reel at frightening speed. I know I must have looked ridiculous trying to run in the water. I was out neck-deep and holding my rod straight overhead when the fish finally turned away from seaward and started angling toward the beach. When I eventually beached the fish, I was a good quarter mile down the beach from the pier.

Man, what a thrill it was catching that fish. My biggest regret was in not keeping it. Big reds are not very fit food. So I measured the fish, and then using the length times girth squared and total in inches divided by 800 arrived at a weight of a little over 41 pounds. The formula, by the way, is recognized in fishing circles. Had I kept the fish, photographed it, and had it weighed on a registered scale with the necessary witnesses present, I could have filed a claim for a spinning record in the 10-pound test line class.

But really, after all the fighting thrills that fish gave me, it had a right to live. In my younger days when I was something of a game hog, I most certainly would have kept it.

I'll guarantee that once a fellow has a battle with big red he won't forget it. Especially so if the catch is made from the surf.

Glossary

ANTI-BACKLASH—A device to keep a reel from overspooling in order to minimize line tangling on reel spool.

BACK BAYS—Water areas located behind barrier reefs, islands, and peninsulas.

BACKLASH—Tangling of line caused by over-running of reel spool.

BAIL—Line pickup device on spinning reel.

BAITFISH—Any type of small fish used as bait for larger fish.

BALANCED TACKLE—General term meaning all parts of fishing gear (rod, reel, line, etc.) work together in harmony.

BARBEL—Whisker-like feelers on chin or around the mouth of fish.

BARREL SWIVEL—A swivel with eyes at each end to join line and leader.

BAY—An inlet of the sea resembling, but smaller than, a gulf.

BIRD'S NEST—Same as a backlash.

BOBBER—Small cork or plastic float used to keep bait off the bottom.

BOTTOM FEEDERS—Fish species that feed on or near the bottom.

BREAKER—When wave curls over and breaks into mass of rushing white water.

BUTT—Lower section of rod; also called rod handle.

CHUM—Extra bait thrown in water to attract fish.

CURRENT—Movement of water caused by tide and/or the wind.

CUTTYHUNK—Linen fishing line; name comes from Cuttyhunk Island, Mass.

DORSAL FIN—The fin on the back of a fish.

DRAG—Reel device to increase or decrease line tension when fighting a fish; also unnatural motion of lure or bait in the water.

DROP—A staging on the leader to which hook is attached.

ECOLOGY—Mutual relationship between organisms and their environment.

EDDY—Small whirlpool caused on down-current side of submerged obstacles.

ESTUARINE—Pertaining to rivers, passages, inlets where tide meets river currents.

FEMALE FERRULE—Socket part of a ferrule.

FERRULE—Friction joint on a rod to permit disassembling.

FILLET—A piece of fish that is bone-free.

FLATS—Shallow areas that are exposed at low tide but covered with water on flood tide.

FREE-SPOOL REEL—A reel on which the spool runs freely on the cast, while the rest of the mechanism, including the handle, remains stationary.

GAFF—Large, strong hook mounted on a handle for the purpose of landing large fish.

GAMEFISH—Species of fish sought more for sport than food.

GANG HOOKS—Hooks fastened together so that the points can be effective from all directions.

GILLS—Organs through which fish can absorb oxygen from the water.

GUIDES—Eyelets through which line runs along a rod.

HORSE—A slang expression used when fish is pulled in by sheer strength.

INSHORE—Close to shore or toward the shore.

JETTY—Wood or wood and rock structure built out from the shore.

JIG—An artificial lure with a lead-head and feather or bristle tail.

LANDING NET—Strong metal hoop with cone-shaped mesh bag for quick landing of fish.

LEADER—Material used between line and hook to minimize visibility or to prevent the fish from cutting line with teeth.

LEVELWIND—A reel device that moves back and forth on retrieve to lay line evenly on the spool.

LIVE BOX—Container in which live bait is kept alive.

LURE—Any kind of artificial bait used in fishing.

MALE FERRULE—Insert part of a ferrule.

MONOFILAMENT—Single strand or solid line.

OAR—A paddle-shaped lever used in rowing a boat.

OFFSHORE—Far from shore or away from shore.

PANFISH—A fish that is caught mainly for eating rather than sport; small size fish that require several to fill a pan.

PLANKTON—Minute animal and plant life that lives in the surface layers of water.

PLAYING A FISH—Act of fighting a hooked fish to tire it out for landing.

PLUGS—Artificial lures made in various shapes and colors from wood and plastic.

POUND TEST—Standard method of classifying line. It is a term used to indicate the dead weight that a line will support.

PROPAGATION—Breeding of fish to increase the species.

REEL SEAT—Metal seat on butt section of rod to which the reel is attached.

RIG—Fishing equipment including rod, reel, line, and terminal tackle.

RUN—When hooked fish moves away from or toward the fisherman.

SAND BAR—Place where currents and waves deposit sand to make water shallower than surrounding area.

SAND SPIKE—A metal tube-like device used in surf fishing to hold rod.

SET—The bend or curvature of the rod tip; also designates driving of hook deep into flesh of fish.

SCHOOLS OF FISH—Concentration of fish all of the same species.

SHANK—Portion of hook extending from eye to bend.

SHOAL—A shallow water area.

SILT—Fine earthy sediment carried and deposited by water.

SINKER—Lead weight used to keep bait and terminal tackle in place in water.

SPAWN—The eggs of fish.

SPIN CASTING—A method of casting in which the line peels off a stationary spool, similar to that of pulling line from one end of a sewing thread spool.

SPOON—A metal artificial lure made in the general shape of a spoon.

STAGING—See DROP.

STAR DRAG—Term applied to star-shaped adjustment on reel to increase or decrease tension on line when fighting a fish.

STRIKE—When fish takes the bait or lure; also act of fisherman setting the hook when the fish grabs bait or lure.

SWIVEL—Connecting device between line and leader to permit

terminal tackle to spin without any resulting twist being put into the line proper.

TERMINAL TACKLE—Term applied to all tackle at end of line.

THUMB STALL—A device on reel against which thumb is pressed to prevent it from over-spooling.

TIDEWATER—Parts of any body of water connected with the sea, such as bays, rivers, inlets, etc., that show the effects of the tide.

TIP TOP—An end guide at the tip end of fishing rod.

TRASH FISH—Fish with neither game nor food value.

TROLLING—Act of dragging a bait or lure through water behind a slowly moving boat.

TROUGH—A depression that runs parallel between sandbars; also called slue or slough.

TYRO—A novice or beginner.

WINDINGS—The wrappings that keep guides, tip topes, etc. firmly affixed to fishing rod.

Bibliography

Considerable technical information as well as specific laws and regulations pertaining to redfish can be obtained from state agencies within the range of the fish. Most of the publications are free.

ALABAMA—Game & Fish Division, Alabama Department of Conservation, Montgomery, Alabama 36104.

DELAWARE—Board of Game and Fish Commissioners, Dover, Delaware 19901.

FLORIDA—Game & Fish Commission, Tallahassee, Florida 32304.

GEORGIA—Game & Fish Commission, State Capitol Building, Atlanta, Georgia 30302.

LOUISIANA—Wildlife & Fisheries Commission, 400 Royal Street, New Orleans, Louisiana 70130.

MARYLAND—Department of Game & Fish, State Office Building, Annapolis, Maryland 21404.

MISSISSIPPI—State Game & Fish Commission, P.O. Box 451, Jackson, Mississippi 39205.

NEW JERSEY—New Jersey State Division of Fish & Game, Box 1809, Trenton, New Jersey 08607.

NORTH CAROLINA—Wildlife Resources Commission, Raleigh, North Carolina 27602.

SOUTH CAROLINA—Wildlife Resources Department, Box 167, Columbia, South Carolina 29202.

TEXAS—Parks & Wildlife Department, John Reagan Building, Austin, Texas 78701.

VIRGINIA—Commission of Game and Fish, Box 1642, Richmond, Virginia 23213.

All of the state agencies listed publish monthly magazines that from time to time carry descriptive and technical articles on redfish. Subscription prices for these magazines range from $5 to $7.50 a year.

BOOKS

Ackerman, Bill. *Handbook of Fishes of The Atlantic Seaboard.* Washington, D.C.: The American Publishing Co., 1957.

Bauer, Erwin A. *The Salt-Water Fisherman's Bible.* Garden City, N.Y.: Doubleday & Co., Inc., 1962.

Becker, A. C., Jr. *Gulf Coast Fishing.* Cranbury, N.J.: A. S. Barnes & Co., Inc., 1970.

————. *Lure Fishing.* Cranbury, N.J.: A. S. Barnes & Co., Inc., 1970.

Camp, Raymond. *Fishing The Surf.* Boston: Little, Brown & Co., 1950.

Evanoff, Vlad. *Fishing Secrets of The Experts.* Garden City, N.Y.: Doubleday & Co., Inc., 1962.

————. *1001 Fishing Tips and Tricks.* New York: Harper & Row, 1966.

————. *How to Fish in Salt Water.* New York: A. S. Barnes & Co., Inc., 1962.

————. *Natural Salt Water Fishing Baits.* New York: A. S. Barnes & Co., Inc., 1953.

————. *Surf Fishing.* New York: A. S. Barnes & Co., Inc., 1951.

Farrington, Chisie. *Women Can Fish.* New York: Coward-McCann Inc., 1951.

Francis, Phil. *Salt Water Fishing From Maine to Texas.* New York: Macmillan Co., 1963.

Francis, Phil and Fichter, George S. *A Guide to Fresh and Salt-Water Fishing.* New York: Golden Press, 1965.

Heilner, Van Campen. *Salt Water Fishing.* New York: Alfred A. Knopf, 1945.

Honea, John W. *Night Fishing in Texas.* San Antonio, Texas: Naylor Co., 1955.

Major, Harlan. *Basic Fishing.* New York: Funk & Wagnalls Co., 1947.

Major, Harlan. *Salt Water Fishing Tackle.* New York: Funk & Wagnalls Co., 1939.

Rodman, O. H. P. *A Handbook of Salt-Water Fishing.* New York: J. B. Lippincott Co., 1952.

Rosko, Milton. *Fishing From Boats.* New York: Macmillan Co., 1964.

Scharff, Robert. *Standard Handbook of Salt-Water Fishing.* New York: Thomas Y. Crowell Co., 1966.

Stilwell, Hart. *Hunting and Fishing in Texas.* New York: Alfred A. Knopf, 1946.

Sylvester, Jerry. *Salt Water Fishing Is Easy.* Harrisburg, Pa.: The Stackpole Co., 1956.

Sportsmen's Encyclopedia. New York: Forest & Stream Publishing Co., 1923.

Westman, James. *Why Fish Bite.* Englewood Cliffs, N.J.: Prentice-Hall, Inc., 1961.

Wulff, Lee (editor). *The Sportsman's Companion.* New York: Harper & Row, 1968.

Index